Prairie

A North American Guide

A BUR OAK GUIDE

Prairie

A North American Guide

Suzanne Winckler

University of Iowa Press **Ψ** Iowa City

University of Iowa Press, Iowa City 52242
Printed in the United States of America
International Standard Book Number 0-87745-883-9

http://www.uiowa.edu/uiowapress

The University of Iowa Press is a member of Green
Press Initiative and is committed to preserving natural
resources. This book has been printed on paper that is
60 percent recycled. GPI is a nonprofit program dedicated to saving trees and natural resources through
increasing the use of recycled paper in the book-
publishing sector.

All efforts have been made to insure the accuracy
of information in this guide; however, note that
acreages, Web addresses, phone numbers, access, and
even highway numbers may change over time.

Printed on acid-free paper

CIP data on file with the Library of Congress

04   05   06   07   08   P   5   4   3   2   1

As to scenery (giving my own thought and feeling),
while I know the standard claim is that Yosemite,
Niagara Falls, the Upper Yellowstone, and the like afford
the greatest natural shows, I am not so sure but that the
prairies and plains, while less stunning at first sight,
last longer, fill the esthetic sense fuller, precede all the rest,
and make North America's characteristic landscape.

—WALT WHITMAN, *Specimen Days*, 1879

CONTENTS

INTRODUCTION

North America's grasslands once stretched from southern Canada to northern Mexico. Across this considerable space, different prairie types—tallgrass, mixed grass, etc.—evolved to express the sum of their particular longitude, latitude, soils, landforms, and aspect. Their ecological characters were shaped as well by the random patterns of grazing animals and fire. This prairie guide is your road map to what remains of a varied and majestic landscape.

In the simplest of terms, prairie grasses decrease in height from east to west in response to decreasing rainfall and increasing evapotranspiration. But soil composition and the lay of the land determine prairie character as well. Sandy soils, cherty soils, blacksoils—each produces its own variation on the grassland theme, so that prairie growing in a low, poorly drained squishy place is not at all like prairie growing on the top of a hill or on the north- or south-facing slope of that very same hill. Over the course of the seasons, every prairie is a progression of growth and decay, a kaleidoscope of ever-changing colors and textures, as different species of grasses and wildflowers wax and wane. These are the reasons why no two prairies are alike and why any given prairie presents a new face with the passing seasons.

A very good way to envision the true and vast scope of North America's grasslands is to consider a cultural map of the Plains Indians (an excellent account can be found in chapter 3 of Walter Prescott Webb's *The Great Plains*). As Webb explains, eleven nomadic tribes—the Saris, Blackfoot, Gros Ventre, Assiniboin, Crow, Cheyenne, Teton-Dakota, Arapaho, Kiowa-Apache, Kiowa, and Comanche—once occupied a grassland realm extending from southern Canada to northern Mexico. I have chosen to focus this guide on the tallgrass, mixed-grass, and short-grass prairies of southern Canada and the central United States—and readers will get a brief encounter with the desert grasslands found in far west Texas—in part because these are the prairies with which I am most familiar. Also, the central U.S. is comprised primarily of private-lands states, that is, states with a limited amount of publicly accessible land. It is simply more of a challenge to find remnant grasslands in these states compared to the public-lands states of, say, Montana, Wyoming, Colorado, and New Mexico, where many national parks and refuges harbor large swaths of grasslands. Although not a guidebook per se, *The Desert Grassland*, edited by Mitchel McClaran and Thomas Van Devender, will compensate for the absence of Mexico in this guide.

It is an unavoidable fact that almost all of North America's prairies have been tilled, fragmented, or manipulated in some way. Numerous scholarly and popular books and Web sites explain and/or lament the details of this remarkable landscape transformation, so I will do little in the way of lamenting or repeating facts that are readily available elsewhere. (See "Recommended Readings, Web Sites, and Organizations" at the end of this book.) I have also made an effort to avoid ecological terminology that might bewilder a newcomer to prairies.

I have four reasons for compiling this prairie guide.

I want to tell people where prairies are—to provide a handy-size book that gives exact instructions on how to drive up to a prairie, get out, and walk on it. I know from experience how difficult this can be. I have driven many miles across the plains with multiple maps, lists, and memos from colleagues, trying to drive and navigate by myself, and I was pretty discouraged at times. It shouldn't be that difficult.

I want to nudge travelers off the interstates and onto the agrarian landscapes where virtually all of North America's remnant prairies now lie. Most people are totally detached from—and quite a few are mildly contemptuous of—agricultural and rural life. I am puzzled by this lack of curiosity and vaguely patronizing fear of agrarian terrain and cultures. I hope this prairie guide will open a door to the landscapes most people fly over or drive through at breakneck speed in their haste to get somewhere else—landscapes that harbor not only our last prairies but also rich histories of exploration, exploitation, war, and peace, not to mention a real world of small towns, farms, and ranches that functions almost as a parallel universe to the urban and suburban worlds most of us inhabit.

I want to show people, on a series of maps, where the last prairies are, so that readers can easily see how few are left (and where the last ones are clustered). These maps will reveal the places where grassland restoration could have the biggest impact in terms of linking existing prairies to create larger landscapes and corridors. Ecologists already know where these places are. I would like the general reader to begin to think in terms of the power of grassland restoration as a conservation tool. And I would like everyone—prairie novices, biologists, environmentalists, farmers, ranchers, small-town bank presidents, politicians, policymakers, and the CEOs of agribusinesses—to consider that the restoration of large viable prairie landscapes is possible within the context of thriving agricultural economies.

Finally, I want people to discover that prairies are not flat, that each prairie has its own character, and that the joy of prairie lies in its subtlety. It is so easy—too easy—to be swept away by mountain and ocean vistas. A prairie, on the other hand, requests the favor of your closer attention. It does not divulge itself to mere passersby. It asks you to stop, to look longer and more intensely. If you come in May, it invites you to come back in August. It reveals itself slowly, much as does a true and lasting friend.

This guide could best be called a celebration of vestiges. It is the consequence of many blissful hours spent milling about on prairies alone or with my spouse or friends. Out in these wide-open spaces I often experience a peculiar sensation—an expansion in the sternum and an uplifting of arms—as if I am about to fly away. If this prosaic list of prairies leads others onto these landscapes and into similar states of mind, I will consider my task a success.

Acknowledgments

Kathy Bolin, a soil scientist in Rochester, Minnesota, showed me how to look at prairies. The following people inspired my continued understanding of grasslands and/or provided critical comments on portions of this text: Holly Carver, Brent Lathrop, Gene Mack, Dan Michener, David Riskin, Vince Shay, David Smith, Al Steuter, Art Thompson, Tom Wendt, and Bill and Jan Whitney.

How to Use This Guide

To find the prairies listed in this guide, you will need two basic accessories: a good map of whatever state or province you plan to visit and a functioning odometer in your car, preferably one that measures miles to the tenths. In addition, patience is a virtue on the mazes of back roads whereon most of today's prairie remnants lie. The publisher and I have made every effort to insure that driving directions are correct; however, please note that changes will occur over time. Field guides to grasses, wildflowers, birds, geology, history, and anthropology will of course enhance your travels. Within each state or province, the prairie sites are listed and numbered on their respective maps in a northwest to southeast direction, and relative sizes of the sites are indicated by symbols. Interstate and trans-Canada highways and state and provincial capitals are also shown.

Prairie

A North American Guide

SASKATCHEWAN   MANITOBA

● < 1,000 acres
○ 1,000–10,000 acres
◉ 10,000–100,000 acres
✛ > 100,000 acres

CANADA

Alberta, Saskatchewan, Manitoba, and Ontario are the prairie provinces of Canada. This guide will focus on grassland remnants in the heart of this region, in Saskatchewan and Manitoba.

Prairie destruction is not constrained by political boundaries, and Canadians have been no kinder to their grasslands than U.S. citizens have. Mixed-grass prairie—the dominant grassland type in Canada—once covered 59 million acres. An estimated 24 percent of that remains, half of it overgrazed. Fescue prairie, which occurred in the northerly, wetter fringes around the mixed-grass prairie, has been reduced to less than 5 percent of its former range. And the tallgrass prairie, centered in the Red River Valley of Manitoba and in southern Ontario, has shrunk to a fraction of 1 percent of its original extent.

The writer Wallace Stegner, who grew up on the Saskatchewan-Alberta border, has written eloquently of the Canadian prairie (and its swift demise) in *Wolf Willow: A History, a Story, and a Memory of the Last Plains Frontier.* Like many lovers of prairie, he is defensive of its subtlety: "The very scale, the hugeness of simple forms, emphasizes stability. It is not hills and mountains which we should call eternal. Nature abhors an elevation as much as it abhors a vacuum; a hill is no sooner elevated than the forces of erosion begin tearing it down. These prairies are quiescent, close to static; looked at for any length of time, they begin to impose their awful perfection on the observer's mind."

SASKATCHEWAN

1 Last Mountain Lake National Wildlife Area
38,530 acres, Canadian Wildlife Service, (306) 836-2022
Mixed-grass prairie and wetland complex along northern reaches of Last Mountain Lake, long recognized for importance to breeding and migratory birds. Dedicated in 1887. Considered North America's first federal bird sanctuary. One-hour driving tour, two nature trails, and

observation tower near National Wildlife Area office and information kiosk.

In Simpson, look for large brown National Wildlife Area sign. Go east 8.5 miles on gravel road, then south 1.8 miles to headquarters.

2 Grasslands National Park

118,745 acres, PC, (306) 298-2257

The only place in Canada where colonies of black-tailed prairie dogs can be found in their native habitat. Mixed-grass prairies in two distinct geological landscapes: 70,222-acre West Block amid glacial plateaus and coulees of Frenchman River Valley and 48,523-acre East Block set in dramatically eroded Killdeer Badlands. West Block has well-marked driving tour and is geared to visitors.

West Block: From visitors' center in Val Marie, go 9 miles east on Highway 18, then 2.5 miles south. East Block: Contact park staff for access information.

MANITOBA

3 Riding Mountain National Park

734,640 acres, PC, (204) 848-7275

Prairie meets boreal forest along the ancient western shoreline of Glacial Lake Agassiz. One of the best places in the province to see elk, black bears, plains bison, moose, coyotes, and beavers. Abundance of hiking, climbing, and horseback riding trails and great birding.

Park headquarters at Wasagaming on Highway 10, which bisects park.

4 Spruce Woods Provincial Park

66,593 acres, PC, (204) 945-6784, (800) 214-6497

Mosaic of white spruce and aspen parkland, riparian hardwoods, sand dunes, and mixed-grass prairie along Assiniboine River. Favorite haunt of nineteenth-century naturalist and Boy Scouts founder Ernest Thompson Seton. Diverse four-season recreational opportunities.

From Brandon, go east 25 miles on Trans-Canada Highway, then south 17 miles on Provincial Trunk Highway 5 to park entrance.

5 Souris River Bend Wildlife Management Area

5,424 acres, MC, (204) 945-6666
Aspen-oak woodlands interspersed with mixed-grass prairie along deeply incised elbow-bend of Souris River Valley.

From Brandon, go 19 miles south on Provincial Trunk Highway 10, go east 4 miles on Provincial Trunk Highway 2 to junction of Provincial Road 346. Go south on Provincial Road 346 (forms western boundary of wildlife management area) and follow designated-vehicle trails.

6 Birds Hill Provincial Park

8,673 acres, MC, (204) 945-6784, (800) 214-6497
Aspen-oak parkland, bogs, and mixed-grass and dry ridge prairies on glacial esker overlooking Red River Valley. Bicycling, hiking, snowshoeing, cross-country skiing, and snowmobiling trails plus the Winnipeg Folk Festival each July. Proximity to Winnipeg means throngs, especially in summer.

From Winnipeg, take Provincial Trunk Highway 59 north 14.9 miles to west entrance gate.

7 Oak Hammock Marsh Wildlife Management Area

8,645 acres, MC, (204) 467-3000
Marshlands, about a tenth of original size, that harbor two tallgrass prairie remnants, totaling about 280 acres. Impressive numbers of migratory waterfowl in spring and fall. A conservation center houses an interpretive center and serves as headquarters for Ducks Unlimited Canada. Dens in nearby Narcisse have the world's largest concentration of red-sided garter snakes.

From Winnipeg, at junction of Perimeter Highway 101 and Provincial Trunk Highway 7, take Provincial Trunk Highway 7 north 11 miles. Go east 5 miles on Provincial Trunk Highway 67, then north 2.5 miles on Provincial Road 220 to parking lot on west edge of marsh.

8 Lake Francis Wildlife Management Area

16,000 acres, MC, (204) 642-6070

Aspen parkland, beach ridges, wetlands, and about 2,000 acres of tall-grass prairie. Lake Francis is a component of the Delta Heritage Marsh, a major breeding and staging area for waterfowl.

From Winnipeg, at junction of Perimeter Highway 101 and Provincial Trunk Highway 6, take Provincial Trunk Highway 6 northwest 19 miles, go west 10 miles on Provincial Road 411.

9 Manitoba Tall Grass Prairie Preserve

6,000 acres, Critical Wildlife Habitat Program, (204) 425-3229

A treasure. Encompasses largest remnant tracts of tallgrass prairie in Canada's Red River Valley and protects several endangered orchid species, including one of the largest known populations in North America of western prairie fringed orchid.

In northwestern Minnesota, take U.S. Highway 59 about 5 miles north across the U.S.-Canada border, go east 2 miles on Provincial Road 209. Preserve properties are between the towns of Tolstoi and Gardenton and are identified with Critical Wildlife Habitat Program signs. Preserve's north block is north of junction of Provincial Roads 209 and 201.

10 Living Prairie Museum

30 acres, City of Winnipeg, (204) 832-0167

Remnant tallgrass prairie, self-guided trails, and interpretive center located at 2795 Ness Avenue in northwest Winnipeg.

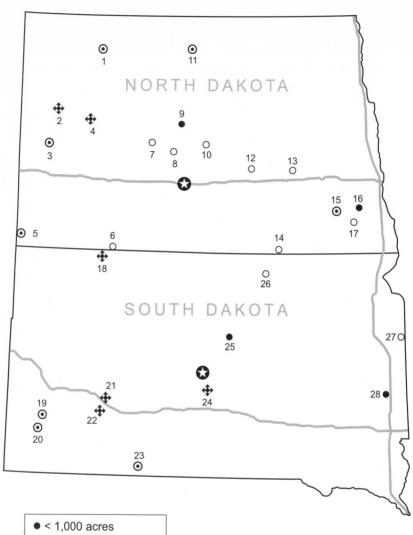

NORTH DAKOTA

SOUTH DAKOTA

● < 1,000 acres
○ 1,000–10,000 acres
◉ 10,000–100,000 acres
✛ > 100,000 acres

THE DAKOTAS

A physiographic map of the Dakotas is a lovely thing to behold. Arcing northwest to southeast across the two states is the Missouri River, the legendary pathway of the Lewis and Clark expedition. Cozying up along the eastern flank of the river is the Missouri Coteau. This impressive landform, which stretches from the Dakotas northwestward through Montana and Saskatchewan to the vicinity of Edmonton, Alberta, is the high, hummocky consequence of immense glaciers that stalled and stagnated while attempting to advance over steep escarpments. (A smaller-scale example of glacial stagnation found in southeastern South Dakota and adjacent parts of Minnesota is called the Prairie Coteau.)

The Missouri Coteau is the most distinctive vestige of the western bounds of continental glaciation. Unfurling to the east are "young" glacial plains, a pothole-marked, poorly drained landscape that segues into the pancake-flat Red River Valley, which is really part of the bed of Glacial Lake Agassiz. West of the Missouri Coteau lies an undulating plain where water has had time to leave a more corrosive mark on the landscape than it has in the glacial drift to the east. Besides numerous streams and rivers cutting paths to the Missouri River, there are the badlands, where water and wind have etched clays and siltstones into bizarre formations.

NORTH DAKOTA

1 Lostwood National Wildlife Refuge
26,900 acres, USFWS, (701) 848-2722
Premier example of Missouri Coteau prairie pothole landscape. Much of refuge is virgin short- and mixed-grass prairie. Auto tour approximately 7 miles long. Naturalist Scott Weidensaul writes of visiting Lostwood in *Living on the Wind: Across the Hemisphere with Migratory Birds* and "wandering its backcountry in a happy trance."

From Stanley, go north 21 miles on Highway 8 to refuge entrance.

2 Little Missouri National Grassland

1.2 million acres, USDA-FS, McKenzie Ranger District, (701) 842-2393;
Medora Ranger District, (701) 225-5151
Subtleties of mixed-grass prairie compete with eye-popping badlands, creating landscape that has made a big impression on countless visitors, including the young Teddy Roosevelt. Hikers and horseback riders can strike out on the 120-mile-long Maah Daah Hey Trail, which begins at Sully Creek State Park south of Medora. A 58-mile self-guided auto tour of the grassland begins at the Medora office.

Information and maps at McKenzie office, 1 mile south of Watford City on Highway 85; Medora office, 161 21st Street West in Dickinson.

3 Theodore Roosevelt National Park

70,447 acres, NPS, south unit, (701) 623-4466; north unit,
(701) 842-2337
See description above. The north and south units of the national park lie within the Little Missouri National Grassland boundaries.

North unit: From Watford City, go south 15 miles on Highway 85 to park entrance. South unit: On I-94, take Exit 27 to Medora Visitor Center or Exit 32 to Painted Canyon Visitor Center.

4 Little Missouri State Park

5,900 acres, NDPRD, (701) 794-3731
Mixed-grass prairie amid dramatically eroded landscape surrounding confluence of Little Missouri and Missouri Rivers, which is now submerged in Sakakawea Reservoir. Best interior access is by horseback.

From Killdeer, go 16 miles north on Highway 22, then east 3 miles on gravel road.

5 Big Gumbo

20,000 acres, Bureau of Land Management, (701) 225-9148
Vast mixed-grass prairie and sagebrush. Named after the state's largest exposure of "gumbo" shale.

From Marmarth, go .25 mile west on Highway 12, then south 18 miles on West River (Camp Crook) Road. Roads are impassable in wet weather.

6 Cedar River National Grassland

6,717 acres, USDA-FS, (605) 374-3592
Rolling hills of mixed-grass prairie. Much of the land lies within the Standing Rock Indian Reservation.

Information and maps at district office, 1005 5th Avenue West, Lemmon, South Dakota.

7 Knife River Indian Villages National Historic Site

1,758 acres, NPS, (701) 745-3309
Mixed-grass prairie at confluence of Knife and Missouri Rivers provides backdrop for three former Hidatsa villages. Site of Lewis and Clark's first encounter in 1804 with Sakakawea. Visitors' center with museum and walking tour.

From Stanton, go north .5 mile on Highway 200A.

8 Cross Ranch Preserve and Cross Ranch State Park

Preserve: 6,000 acres, TNC, (701) 794-8741; State Park: 589 acres, NDPRD, (701) 794-3731
Superb example of northern mixed-grass prairie and floodplain forest along relatively wild stretch of the much-garroted Missouri River.

From Bismarck, go north about 33 miles on Highway 1806.

9 John E. Williams Prairie

1,601 acres, TNC, (701) 794-8741
Stark prairiescape (locals call the site Valley-of-the-Moon) encompassing alkaline lake and salt-encrusted mudflats. To add to starkness, TNC advises visitors of periodic presence of high winds and wood ticks. Supports large nesting population of threatened piping plovers. Because public access is limited during the breeding season, please contact TNC prior to visiting.

From Turtle Lake, go east and then north 3 miles on Highway 41, then east 3 miles on County Road 27. Where County Road 27 turns north, continue on gravel road, which will jog south briefly, then turn east. Go 2 miles. Preserve entrance is on south side of road.

10 Davis Ranch

7,017 acres, TNC, (701) 222-8464

Impressive expanse of mixed-grass prairie and pothole wetlands on breathtakingly empty Missouri Coteau. Preserve is leased for cattle grazing; visitors are advised to leave gates closed or opened as they find them. Contact TNC regarding access.

From Wing, go north 15.5 miles on Highway 14. Take gravel road to west .5 to 1.5 miles to designated parking areas.

11 J. Clark Salyer National Wildlife Refuge

59,000 acres, USFWS, (701) 768-2548

Straddles 50-mile stretch of Souris River; southern portion of refuge encompasses extensive sandhill prairie once the bed of an ancient glacial lake. Auto trails 5 and 22 miles long, 13-mile canoe trail (a designated National Recreation Trail), observation towers for photography and birdwatching. Refuge name honors J. Clark Salyer, chief of the Division of Wildlife Refuges, U.S. Fish and Wildlife Service, from 1934 to 1961.

From Towner, go about 22 miles northwest on Highway 14.

12 Chase Lake National Wildlife Refuge

4,385 acres, USFWS, (701) 752-4218

Unfurling prairie, dotted with pothole wetlands, surrounds large alkaline lake on the Missouri Coteau. Refuge is also a federally designated wilderness area. In summer, harbors 10,000 to 12,000 white pelicans, largest nesting colony of this species in North America. Much of the surrounding land remains in grassland, making this site one of the largest areas of native prairie in North Dakota.

From Medina, go north 10 miles on County Road 68 (55th Avenue Southeast), west 3 miles, north 2 miles, west 4.5 miles, then south 3 miles.

13 Edward M. Brigham III Sanctuary

2,200 acres, NAS, (701) 298-3373
Classic prairie pothole landscape encompassing permanent brackish lake and seventy small evanescent potholes amid upland prairie. Excellent site for viewing sharp-tailed grouse.

From Jamestown, go north 8 miles on Highway 20, east 4 miles on gravel road, then .5 mile north.

14 Johnson's Gulch Wildlife Management Area

1,402 acres, NDPRD, (701) 683-4900
Prairie uplands and wooded ravines on eroded eastern flank of Missouri Coteau. One of the best areas in central and east North Dakota for imagining the prairie landscape as it appeared before statehood.

From Kulm, take Highway 56 south 21 miles to Highway 11, go east .7 mile, then south 2 miles and east 2 miles on gravel road to parking area.

15 Sheyenne National Grassland

70,180 acres, USDA-FS, (701) 683-4342
Tallgrass and mixed-grass prairie within the Sheyenne Delta, ancient dune field on edge of Glacial Lake Agassiz. Area contains largest extant examples of tallgrass prairie in Red River Valley. Also has state's largest greater prairie-chicken population and many recreational opportunities.

Grassland is about 30 miles southwest of Fargo. Information and maps at district office in Lisbon at junction of Highway 32 and Highway 27.

16 Pigeon Point Preserve

600 acres, TNC, (701) 222-8464
Spring-fed wetlands, fens, and prairie along Sheyenne River. A superb concentration of biodiversity.

From junction of Highway 18 and Highway 27, go west 10 miles on Highway 27, north 4 miles on 147th Avenue Southeast, then west 2 miles to preserve entrance.

17 Brown Ranch

1,531 acres, TNC, (701) 439-0841

Virtually undisturbed tallgrass prairie on sandy uplands intermingling with wet swales. Ranch is bordered on two sides by Sheyenne National Grassland.

From McLeod, go west and south about 8 miles on gravel road to first four-way intersection. Go west 2 miles, then north .1 mile to office.

SOUTH DAKOTA

18 Grand River National Grassland

155,000 acres, USDA-FS, (605) 374-3592

Rolling mixed-grass prairie and badlands. Abundant opportunities for hunting, fishing, and camping.

Located on the South Dakota–North Dakota border. Major north-south routes through the grassland include Highway 75, County Road 9, and Highway 73. For maps and information, contact district office, 1005 5th Avenue West, in Lemmon.

19 Custer State Park

73,000 acres, South Dakota Department of Game, Fish and Parks, (605) 255-4515

This huge, economically self-sufficient park (it does not rely on taxpayer dollars) is best known for its scenic expanses of rugged, pine-clad mountains; however, intermingled within the forests are 8,000 acres of mixed-grass prairie. Campgrounds, guided nature walks, living-history demonstrations, 18-mile auto trail. Park supports a herd of 1,400 bison.

From Custer, go east about 8 miles on Highway 16.

20 Wind Cave National Park

28,295 acres, NPS, (605) 745-4600

Extensive mixed-grass prairie that should receive equal billing with Wind Cave, one of the world's longest and most complex caves, as a major attraction.

From Hot Springs, go north 7 miles on Highway 385.

21 Buffalo Gap National Grassland

591,000 acres in scattered tracts, USDA-FS, Fall River Ranger District, (605) 745-4107; Wall Ranger District, (605) 279-2125

Immense area encompassing gamut of prairie types (tallgrass, mixed-grass, short-grass), woody ravines, and badlands formations. Fall River Unit is in southwest corner of state; Wall Unit is on east end of Badlands National Park. National Grasslands Visitor Center, in Wall, provides an overview of federal grasslands.

Contact ranger districts for maps and information.

22 Badlands National Park

244,000 acres, NPS, (605) 433-5361

Wind- and water-sculpted wonderland of bizarre landforms amid which lies the largest protected mixed-grass prairie in U.S. Black-footed ferrets have been reintroduced in 64,000-acre Badlands Wilderness Area within the park.

From I-80, take Wall exit (110) and go south on Highway 240 (Badlands Loop Road).

23 Lacreek National Wildlife Refuge

16,410 acres, USFWS, (605) 685-6508

Wetlands, wet meadows, and upland grasslands on fringe of Nebraska Sandhills, which barely creep across the border into South Dakota. About 4,900 acres within refuge is native prairie, most of which (3,726 acres) contains vegetation typical of the Sandhills.

From Martin, go south 4 miles on Highway 73, east 1 mile, south 1 mile, then east 7 miles to refuge headquarters.

24 Fort Pierre National Grassland

116,000 acres, USDA-FS, (605) 224-5517

Mixed-grass prairie unfurls across miles of rolling hills and swales. Known for its vigorous populations of greater prairie-chicken and sharp-tailed grouse; blinds in spring allow views of the male birds' elaborate booming rituals. While most national grasslands are in remote areas, this grassland is easily accessible from Pierre on the north and I-90 on the south.

Highway 83 is primary north-south route through grassland. From Pierre, go south about 8 miles to northern boundary. From I-90, take Exit 212 and go north about 5 miles to southern boundary. For maps and information, contact the district office, 124 S. Euclid Avenue, in Pierre.

25 E.M. and Ida Young Preserve

901 acres, TNC, (605) 342-4040
Mixed-grass prairie and wetlands.

From Agar, go east about 9 miles. Located immediately north of Cottonwood Lake. Contact TNC for visitation information.

26 Samuel H. Ordway, Jr., Memorial Prairie

7,800 acres, TNC, (605) 439-3475
Blend of tallgrass and mixed-grass prairie perched on the Missouri Coteau. Long-established TNC preserve that supports herd of 250 bison. Self-guided nature trail.

From Leola, go west about 8 miles on Highway 10. Nature trail area is 1 mile west of blue water tower. Preserve on south side of road. Look for address on mailbox, 35333 115th Street.

27 Crystal Springs

2,290 acres, TNC, (605) 874-8517
Tallgrass prairie and wetlands on Altamont moraine, glacial feature on a finger of Prairie Coteau that extends into South Dakota from Minnesota. TNC provides conservation management for this privately owned property.

From Clear Lake, go 1 mile north on Highway 15, east 3 miles on county road, 1 mile north, 1 mile east, 1 mile north, then 1.5 miles east to parking area on south side of road, located just before Monighan Creek crossing. Contact TNC for visitation information.

28 Sioux Prairie

200 acres, TNC, (605) 874-8517
Tallgrass prairie and potholes.

From intersection of I-29 and Highway 34 east of Colman, go west 1.5 miles on Highway 34, then north 3.5 miles on Highway 77. Preserve is on east side of road.

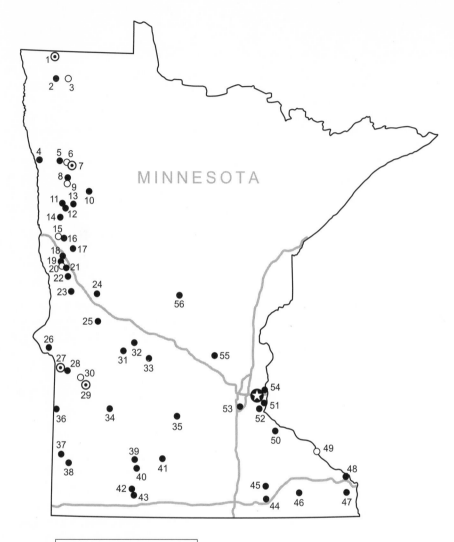

MINNESOTA

● < 1,000 acres
○ 1,000–10,000 acres
⊙ 10,000–100,000 acres

MINNESOTA

In Minnesota, it is hard to say "prairie" without saying "Glacial Lake Agassiz" in the same breath. This immense body of water was formed by retreating ice sheets during the last period of glaciation some ten thousand years ago. According to Warren Upham, the nineteenth-century geologist who surveyed and described it, Glacial Lake Agassiz in its prime was about 700 miles long and 250 miles wide and covered an area of about 110,000 square miles (by comparison, the entire state of Minnesota is 86,943 square miles). The huge handprint left behind by Glacial Lake Agassiz—in the form of deltas, drift deposits, moraines, and beach ridges of gravel and sand—is associated with many prairies in western Minnesota as well as in adjacent areas of North Dakota and Canada.

Today, the shallow, undulating basin of Glacial Lake Agassiz contains some of the finest remnant tallgrass prairie in the country; it is also an active area of prairie conservation and restoration. Though I grew up in the grassland state of Texas, it was not until I lived in Minnesota and visited Glacial Lake Agassiz that I began to understand what a prairie really is. I wish the same good fortune to other prairie novices.

1 Wallace C. Dayton Conservation and Wildlife Area
13,000 acres, TNC, (218) 436-3455
With several surrounding state wildlife management areas, this preserve takes in an impressive scope of tallgrass aspen parkland, one of many discrete prairie regions within the ancient bed of Glacial Lake Agassiz. Tallgrass aspen parkland encompasses about 1.2 million acres of aspen and balsam poplar woodlands intermingled with prairies and fens in northwestern Minnesota and southeastern Manitoba. It is a relatively remote and unpopulated landscape and in summer can demand a high tolerance for biting insects. Nonetheless, one of the exhilarating aspects of this tallgrass aspen parkland is that it has survived into the twenty-first century largely unfragmented. It harbors moose, gray wolves, and rare birds and plants declining in other areas.

From Lancaster, go east 6 miles on County Road 4, then north and watch for Conservation and Wildlife Area signs.

2 Norway Dunes

320 acres, TNC, (612) 331-0750
High-quality savanna of stunted oaks and dry-to-mesic prairie within dune formation on eastern shore of Glacial Lake Agassiz.

From Halma, go east .8 mile on County Road 7, then north 2 miles on gravel road to where a dirt road turns west, at which point go *east* on grassy tract about .5 mile to southwest corner of preserve.

3 Two Rivers Aspen Prairie Parkland

1,333 acres, SNA, www.dnr.state.mn.us/snas
Fine example of tallgrass aspen parkland.

From Karlstad, go east 8 miles on Highway 11, then .5 mile east of Pelan go north for .25 mile.

4 Malmberg Prairie

80 acres, SNA and TNC, www.dnr.state.mn.us/snas
Prairie remnant in flat, poorly drained (not pejorative terms for prairie watchers) southern basin of Glacial Lake Agassiz.

From Crookston, go west 9 miles on County Road 9, then south 2 miles on County Road 56.

5 Pankratz Memorial Prairie

920 acres in two tracts, TNC, (612) 331-0750
Variably wet and mesic prairie sprawling across Glacial Lake Agassiz beach ridges. North (468 acres) and south (452 acres) units separated by about a mile.

From Crookston, go east 6 miles on Highway 2, south 1.5 miles on County Road 46 to west corner of north unit. To south unit, continue south 1.5 miles on County Road 46, then east .5 mile.

6 Pembina Trail Preserve

2,377 acres, SNA and TNC, www.dnr.state.mn.us/snas
A crown jewel of Minnesota prairies. High diversity of grass and wild-flower species. Congregation of sandhill cranes in fall, booming prairie-chickens and sharp-tailed grouse in spring, moose frequent. Pembina Trail was ox-cart trade route between Winnipeg and St. Paul. Preserve is in three units (Crookston Prairie, Pembina Trail, and Foxboro Prairie).
From Mentor, go west 9 miles on County Road 45.

7 Glacial Ridge Project

24,142 acres, TNC, (218) 637-2146
Ambitious, multipartner prairie-wetland restoration project. Ultimately will reconnect existing remnant prairies, such as Pembina Trail Preserve (see site above), and provide unfragmented habitat for a host of grassland-dependent species.
From Crookston, go 12 miles east on Highway 2, then south about 3 miles on Highway 32 to project headquarters.

8 Agassiz Dunes

435 acres, SNA and TNC, www.dnr.state.mn.us/snas
Dune field on shoreline of Glacial Lake Agassiz. Mix of oak savanna, aspen thickets, short-grass and tallgrass prairie. Grand display of pasque flowers in early spring.
From Fertile, go south 1 mile on Highway 32, then west .4 mile on a gravel road.

9 Prairie Smoke Dunes

1,107 acres, SNA, www.dnr.state.mn.us/snas
Rich mix of plant communities amid Glacial Lake Agassiz dunes, including sand savanna, sedge meadow, and wet prairie.
From Twin Valley, go north 14 miles on Highway 32, then west .25 mile on County Road 7.

10 Santee Prairie

442 acres, SNA, www.dnr.state.mn.us/snas
Blacksoil prairie, pothole marshes, sedge meadows.

From Mahnomen, go north 5 miles on Highway 59, then east 2.5 miles.

11 Sandpiper Prairie

320 acres, SNA, www.dnr.state.mn.us/snas
Dry prairie on gravel beach ridges, plus wet and mesic prairies.

From Twin Valley, go west 6.5 miles on County Road 27 past airport, then take gravel road south 1.5 miles.

12 Twin Valley Prairie

499 acres, SNA and TNC, www.dnr.state.mn.us/snas
Dry beach ridge prairie, blacksoil prairie, and marshland. Good wildlife diversity.

From Twin Valley, go south 5 miles on Highway 32, then west 4.5 miles on County Road 39.

13 Frenchman's Bluff

51 acres, SNA and TNC, www.dnr.state.mn.us/snas
Panoramic views of Glacial Lake Agassiz from atop 200-foot glacial moraine. While small in extent, supports diverse flora representative of tallgrass and short-grass prairies. Since 1950s, a study site for the Itasca Biological Station.

From Syre, go east 4 miles on Highway 113, then north 1.1 miles on County Road 36.

14 Felton Prairie Complex

761 acres in four tracts, SNA and TNC, www.dnr.state.mn.us/snas
Four exceptional prairie remnants within large beach ridge complex. The most important gravel prairie complex in the state.

From Felton to Shrike Prairie (90 acres), go east 2 miles on Highway 34, prairie is on north side of road; to Assiniboia Prairie (191 acres), go east 4 miles on Highway 34, then north 1.5 miles on County Road 110; to Blazing Star Prairie (160 acres), go east 4 miles on Highway 34, then

1 mile south on unpaved township road; to Bicentennial Prairie (320 acres), go south 2 miles on Highway 9, then east 2.5 miles on County Road 108.

15 Bluestem Prairie

4,658 acres, SNA and TNC, (218) 498-2679

One of the highest-quality tallgrass prairie remnants in the U.S. Encompasses impressive examples of the Red River Valley's once vast and diverse grasslands, including tallgrass and blacksoil prairies, sedge meadows, and calcareous fen communities. Blinds for viewing greater prairie-chickens in early spring can be reserved.

From Moorhead, go east about 14 miles on Highway 10, south 1.5 miles on Highway 9, then east 1.5 miles on unmarked gravel road.

16 Margherita Preserve/Audubon Prairie

480 acres, TNC, (612) 331-0750

Tallgrass prairie and aspen woodlands in poorly drained soils of lake bed of Glacial Lake Agassiz.

From Hawley, go south 5 miles on County Road 31, then west 3 miles on Township Road 119 (condition of roadway poor for last .25 mile).

17 Blanket Flower Prairie

304 acres, SNA, www.dnr.state.mn.us/snas

Amid rolling hills, dry upland prairie segues into mesic prairie in lower areas.

From Barnesville, go east 8 miles on Highway 34, north 1 mile on Highway 32, east 1 mile on gravel road, then north .75 mile on gravel road.

18 Richard M. and Mathilde Rice Elliot Prairie

497 acres, SNA and TNC, www.dnr.state.mn.us/snas

Flat tallgrass prairie, scattered sedge meadows.

From Rothsay, go northwest about 8 miles on Highway 52 (which parallels I-94), then east 1.5 miles on County Road 188.

19 Western Prairie

320 acres, SNA and TNC, www.dnr.state.mn.us/snas

More flat tallgrass prairie, sedge meadows, wetlands, saline area.

From Rothsay, go west 5 miles on County Road 26, north 4 miles on County Road 15, then west .5 mile on County Road 182.

20 Anna Gronseth Prairie

1,300 acres, TNC, (612) 331-0750

Tallgrass prairie supporting population of greater prairie-chickens.

From Rothsay, go west 5 miles on County Road 26, then south 3.5 miles on County Road 169.

21 Town Hall Prairie

240 acres, TNC, (612) 331-0750

Tallgrass prairie and marshy areas situated on gently sloping terrain that parallels highest beach ridge of Glacial Lake Agassiz. Greater prairie-chicken habitat.

From Rothsay, go west 2 miles on County Road 26, south 4 miles on County Road 19, then west .5 mile on County Road 20.

22 Foxhome Prairie

240 acres, TNC, (612) 331-0750

Impressive tallgrass remnant important for greater prairie-chickens.

From Foxhome, go west .5 mile on Highway 210, north 3 miles on County Road 19, then east 1.5 miles on gravel road.

23 Ottertail Prairie

320 acres, SNA, www.dnr.state.mn.us/snas

Low, wet prairie. Calcareous groundwater influences plant community. May be flooded in wet springs.

South of Fergus Falls, take Exit 55 off I-94, go south 7 miles on County Road 1, then west 6 miles on County Road 112.

24 Seven Sisters Prairie

136 acres, TNC, (612) 331-0750

Seven knolls—hence the name—on the Alexandria moraine overlooking Lake Christina, a migratory waterfowl stop. Commingling of wet and dry prairies creates plant communities that have drawn botanists to the area since the 1890s.

From I-94, take Ashby exit (77), go north on Highway 78 through town. About 3 miles from Ashby, look for prominent ridge on north side of road (Lake Christina is to the south). Park at gated road that leads to gravel pit.

25 Staffanson Prairie

95 acres, TNC, (612) 331-0750

Prairie pothole landscape on western flank of Alexandria moraine.

From Kensington, go north about 1.5 miles on County Road 1, west 2 miles on Wennersburg Road (gravel), then north 1 mile on Unity Drive.

26 Clinton Prairie

160 acres, SNA, www.dnr.state.mn.us/snas

Upland blacksoil prairie on gently undulating moraine.

From Clinton, go west 6 miles on County Road 6.

27 Big Stone National Wildlife Refuge

11,521 acres, USFWS, (320) 273-2191

Wide valley of Minnesota River carved by glacial meltwater encompassing wetlands, woodlands, and 1,700 acres of native tallgrass prairie. Year-round recreational opportunities, 6-mile auto tour, leaflet available at refuge headquarters.

From Ortonville, go southeast 3 miles on Highway 7.

28 Plover Prairie

655 acres in two tracts, TNC, (612) 331-0750

Richly diverse site that combines upland prairie on flat, well-drained rocky terraces overlooking the Minnesota River Valley with wet prairie and cattail marshes on lower ground along the river. The prairie provides habitat for, and takes its name from, a quintessential grassland bird—the upland plover—a graceful, long-necked bird whose plaintive whistles provide one source of pleasure for prairie watching and listening. (Please note the bird's common name was changed some years ago to upland sandpiper.)

From Bellingham, go north about 3 miles on Highway 75, east 2 miles on County Road 38, then north 1 mile to reach larger 516-acre tract. The 139-acre tract is located 4 miles north of Bellingham on east side of Highway 75.

29 Lac Qui Parle Wildlife Management Area

32,000 acres, Minnesota Department of Natural Resources,
(320) 734-4451
Serpentine preserve—25 miles along Minnesota River—that features constructed lakes, river bottom woodlands and wetlands, and numerous large and small tracts of native tallgrass prairie, including a contiguous extension of Chippewa Prairie (see site below) of comparable size. The French name of the site translates as "Lake That Speaks."

From Milan, go southeast 2 miles on Highway 59/7, south 2 miles on County Road 32, then west .25 mile on County Road 33 to headquarters.

30 Chippewa Prairie

1,143 acres, TNC, (605) 874-8517
Large tallgrass prairie remnant associated with important wetlands for migratory waterfowl at Lac Qui Parle Wildlife Management Area (see site above).

From Milan, go northwest about 3 miles on Highway 59/7, then west 2 miles on county line road (gravel).

31 Ordway Prairie

581 acres, TNC, (612) 331-0750
Dry hill prairie, wet prairie, marshes, willow thickets, and calcareous fens, plus lovely vistas from hilltops.

From Brooten, go about 7 miles west on County Road 8, then south 3 miles on Highway 104. Park at pull-off for historical marker.

32 Sedan Brook

191 acres, SNA, www.dnr.state.mn.us/snas
Excellent example of mesic blacksoil prairie.

From Brooten, go north 3 miles on County Road 18, then east .75 mile on County Road 27. Park on north side of road and walk .5 mile on field road to site.

33 Regal Meadow

385 acres, TNC, (612) 331-0750
Sedge meadow and prairie that varies from wet to mesic. A last vestige of a once larger prairiescape on glacial outwash valley of Crow Wing River.

From Paynesville, go southwest 6 miles on Highway 23 to Hawick, then north 2 miles on gravel road.

34 Gneiss Outcrops

241 acres, SNA, www.dnr.state.mn.us/snas
Metamorphic 3.9-billion-year-old gneiss outcrops along the Glacial River Warren Valley support dryland prairie species such as Great Plains prickly pear.

From Granite Falls, go east 1.5 miles on Highway 212, then south 1 mile on County Road 40.

35 Schaefer Prairie

160 acres, TNC, (612) 331-0750
Tallgrass prairie remnant, known for changing array of wildflowers May through September.

From Glencoe, go west 7 miles on Highway 212, then south on gravel road called Nature Avenue (opposite County Road 4). Continue .5 mile to first intersection. Prairie lies to southwest of intersection.

36 Mound Springs Prairie

465 acres, SNA, www.dnr.state.mn.us/snas
Situated in dramatic ocean-swell landscape of Prairie Coteau region that straddles South Dakota–Minnesota border. Diverse dry prairie

atop hills gives way to wet prairie and peculiar domed seepage wetlands (hence Mound Springs) at base of hills.

From Gary, South Dakota, go east .5 mile on County Road 4, then south 1 mile on gravel road. Turn west and park on south side of road.

37 Hole-in-the-Mountain Prairie

590 acres, TNC, (612) 331-0750

Another large prairie remnant on the spectacular Prairie Coteau. Known for summer wildflower displays and high diversity of butterfly species.

From Lake Benton, go south 1.5 miles on Highway 75. Turnout on west side of road.

38 Prairie Coteau

329 acres, SNA, www.dnr.state.mn.us/snas

Lovely swatch of prairie—ranging from high, dry, and gravelly to low and wet—undulates across Bemis glacial moraine. Great views from ridge top.

From Pipestone, go northeast about 10 miles on Highway 23 just north of Holland. Turnout on west side of road.

39 Cottonwood River Prairie

181 acres, SNA, www.dnr.state.mn.us/snas

North- and south-facing slopes demonstrate how aspect affects distribution of prairie plants (some prefer it cool and moist, others hot and dry). More great views.

From Springfield, go west 3 miles on Highway 14, then south 3 miles on County Road 2; after road turns west, continue .5 mile.

40 Red Rock Prairie

611 acres, TNC, (612) 331-0750

Tallgrass prairie amid outcrops of 1.5-billion-year-old Sioux quartzite. Restoration of old fields began in 1994.

From Windom, go north about 15 miles on Highway 71, east 5 miles on County Road 10, then south 1.25 miles on County Road 45 (gravel).

41 Joseph A. Tauer Prairie

80 acres, SNA, www.dnr.state.mn.us/snas

A Guide to Minnesota's Scientific and Natural Areas summarizes Tauer's "eccentric" farming ideas, which included a disinterest in draining lowland areas. He farmed with horses until 1980, preserving this prairie area undisturbed.

From New Ulm, go south 8 miles on Highway 13, then west 2 miles on Highway 22.

42 Des Moines River Prairie

210 acres, SNA, www.dnr.state.mn.us/snas

High-quality example of gravelly hill prairie.

From Windom, go southeast about 3 miles on Highway 71, south 3 miles on County Road 79, then west .5 mile on County Road 30.

43 Holthe Prairie

148 acres, SNA, www.dnr.state.mn.us/snas

Hill prairie and the largest known calcareous fen in the Des Moines River Valley.

From Windom, go southeast 4.5 miles on Highway 71, south 4.5 miles on County Road 19, then west .75 mile on minimum maintenance road.

44 Wild Indigo Prairie

150 acres, SNA, www.dnr.state.mn.us/snas

Fine example of mesic tallgrass prairie along 12-mile stretch of abandoned railroad right-of-way.

Between Dexter and Ramsey. Access at Dexter, or from Dexter go west about 6 miles on Highway 2, then south on County Road 19 where it crosses railroad right-of-way.

45 Iron Horse Prairie

35 acres, SNA, www.dnr.state.mn.us/snas

Triangle of mesic tallgrass prairie between two railroad spurs. High plant species diversity.

From Hayfield, go south 2 miles on Highway 56, then east .5 mile on County Road M to old railroad grade.

46 Pin Oak Prairie

184 acres, SNA, www.dnr.state.mn.us/snas

Wet meadows along Root River shift to dry prairie on bluffs. These are capped with oak forest that undoubtedly has become denser with suppression of fire.

From Chatfield, go 4 miles southwest on County Road 5. Take gravel road south .5 mile and park just past bridge over Middle Branch of Root River on east side of road.

47 Mound Prairie

257 acres, SNA, www.dnr.state.mn.us/snas

Encompasses three goat prairies (so named for steep inclines and south-facing exposure) that afford high species diversity and fine views. Within Richard J. Dorer Memorial Hardwood State Forest.

From Hokah, go west 4 miles on Highway 16. Park on gravel road on north side of highway.

48 King's and Queen's Bluff

178 acres, SNA, (507) 643-6849

Two goat prairies with spectacular views of Mississippi River Valley. Queen's Bluff requires educational-use permit. In O. L. Kipp State Park, just north of the I-90/Highway 61 interchange.

From Winona, take Highway 61 southeast 12 miles to County Road 12 and follow signs to park.

49 Kellogg-Weaver Dunes

1,004 acres, SNA and TNC, www.dnr.state.mn.us/snas

Rolling dunes of intermingled prairie and oak savanna on backwater terrace of Mississippi River.

From Kellogg, go east and south 4.3 miles on County Road 84.

50 Spring Creek Prairie

145 acres, SNA, www.dnr.state.mn.us/snas
Sandstone and limestone bluffs along tributary of Mississippi River. North-facing slopes support oak woodland; southwest-facing slopes are clad with dry prairie.

From Highway 61 on west edge of Red Wing, take Tyler Road south to Red Fox Drive, continuing south to Wild Turkey Lane. Go west and park at end of road.

51 Lost Valley Prairie

200 acres, SNA, www.dnr.state.mn.us/snas
Bluff prairie in the southern oak barrens. One of the few sites in the state where rock sandwort is found.

From Afton on the St. Croix River, go south 3 miles on Highway 21, west .75 mile on County Road 78 (also called 110th Street), then north .5 mile on Nyberg Avenue.

52 Grey Cloud Dunes

220 acres, SNA, www.dnr.state.mn.us/snas
Two sandy terraces rise 60 and 110 feet respectively above the Mississippi River. Dry prairie interspersed with blowouts, exposed sand sculpted by prevailing southwesterly winds.

From Highway 61 in Cottage Grove, exit and go south on Jamaica Avenue, then west on 100th Street, then south on Hadley Avenue. Park at intersection with 103d Street and walk east on field road to prairie.

53 Black Dog Preserve

130 acres, SNA and TNC, (952) 845-5900
Wet and mesic prairies surrounding rare example of calcareous fen, within Minnesota Valley National Wildlife Refuge. Named after Dakota Sioux chief.

In Burnsville (a suburb of Minneapolis), take Exit 4A off I-35W, go east .5 mile on road that goes under I-35 to Cliff Road. Continue .5 mile to parking lot.

54 St. Croix Savanna

112 acres, SNA, www.dnr.state.mn.us/snas

Hill prairie and oak savanna, located within Lower St. Croix National Scenic Riverway.

From Bayport, go south .5 mile on Highway 95. Park on shoulder and look for Scientific and Natural Areas sign.

55 Uncas Dunes

745 acres, SNA, www.dnr.state.mn.us/snas

Oak-prairie savanna amid ancient dune field, within Sand Dunes State Forest. Site named for rare butterfly, the Uncas skipper.

From Zimmerman, go west 4 miles on County Road 4, then south 1.5 miles to campground in state forest.

56 Ripley Esker

236 acres, SNA, www.dnr.state.mn.us/snas

Oak-prairie savanna covers the dry south-facing slope of the esker, a steep-sided, serpentine glacial deposit of sand and gravel. This site is part of a 6.75-mile esker system. Many glacial deposits of this type have been mined for aggregate materials and consequently have become rare landforms.

From Little Falls, go north 7 miles on Highway 371, east .7 mile on County Road 48, then north 1 mile on County Road 282.

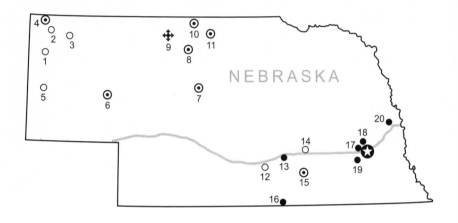

NEBRASKA

I have always thought of Nebraska as the Rockies in repose. The state is a vast depository of rock, gravel, and sand carried off those mountains by a succession of ancient, meandering rivers, of which the most prominent today is the Platte. The rivers' cargo, abandoned on the plain, was then blown and rearranged by the wind. Of course, the geological story of Nebraska is far more complex, and the same erosional processes apply in the other states that lie on the eastern flank of the Rockies. Nevertheless, I cherish Nebraska for giving me mountains the way I like them: lying down and mantled in grass. One of my favorite images of Nebraska comes from Mari Sandoz, who in *Love Song to the Plains* described her native state as "a golden hackberry leaf in the sun, a giant curling, tilted leaf. The veins of it were the long streams rising out near the mountains and flowing eastward to the Big Muddy, the wild Missouri."

1 Agate Fossil Beds National Monument
2,762 acres, NPS, (308) 668-2211
Hotbed of nineteenth-century paleontological research amid mixed-grass prairie near headwaters of Niobrara River.

From Mitchell, go north 34 miles on Highway 29, or from Harrison go south 22 miles on Highway 29.

2 Soldier Creek Wilderness
7,794 acres, USDA-FS, (308) 432-4475, (308) 432-0200
Mixed-grass prairie intermingles with riparian cottonwood savanna and upland ponderosa pine. A variety of trails for hikers and horseback riders.

From Crawford, go west 2.5 miles on Highway 20 to Fort Robinson State Park, then 6 miles north on Soldier Creek Road to trailhead. Maps and information at district office, 1240 W. 16th Street in Chadron.

3 Pine Ridge National Recreation Area

6,600 acres, USDA-FS, (308) 432-4475, (308) 432-0300
Primitive-use and nonmotorized recreation on horseback, hiking, and mountain bike trails through habitats similar to Soldier Creek Wilderness.

Primary access is Roberts Trailhead. From Chadron, go west 8 miles on Highway 20, south 7 miles on Eleson Road, then east 1.5 miles on Bethel Road. Maps and information at district office, 1240 W. 16th Street in Chadron.

4 Oglala National Grassland

94,000 acres, USDA-FS, (308) 432-4475
Vast expanses of badlands and mixed-grass prairie in Nebraska panhandle.

Maps and information at district office, 1240 W. 16th Street in Chadron.

5 Scotts Bluff National Monument

3,000 acres, NPS, (308) 436-4340
Massive sandstone landmark on Oregon Trail, surrounded by mixed-grass prairie. Includes 50-acre prairie restoration of former country club golf course.

From I-80, take Kimball exit (20), go north about 45 miles on Highway 71, then west 2 miles on Highway 92.

THE NEBRASKA SANDHILLS

Approximately 12 million acres

For any aspiring prairie watcher, a visit to Nebraska is mandatory, because the state possesses the largest unfragmented grassland in the U.S. The Sandhills, in north central Nebraska, are roughly three times the size of Massachusetts and comprise the largest dune formation in the Western Hemisphere. Most of the land is in private ownership and ranching is the main livelihood. The Sandhills are a national treasure as a landform and as a place where the culture and economy are in sync with the natural rhythms of the biome.

Numerous paved highways provide vistas of magnificent grasslands and wetlands, including Highway 2 (Thedford to Ellsworth), Highway 27 (Ellsworth to Gordon), Highway 61 (Hyannis to Merriman), Highway 97 (Mullen to Valentine), and Highway 83 (Thedford to Valentine). Public access locations, which allow opportunities for fishing, hunting, birdwatching, and so on, follow for six areas.

6 Crescent Lake National Wildlife Refuge

45,818 acres, USFWS, (308) 762-4893

Remote, exquisite landscape. Two dozen lakes clustered amid grass-covered dunes offer fine example of extensive wetlands found throughout Sandhills.

From Oshkosh, on Highway 26, go north 28 miles on dirt road (W. Second Street).

7 Bessey Ranger District, Nebraska National Forest

90,444 acres, USDA-FS, (308) 533-2257

A 20,000-acre planted forest (the only one in the federal forest system) surrounded by thousands of acres of Sandhills prairie, all open to recreation.

From Halsey, go west about 2 miles on Highway 2.

8 Valentine National Wildlife Refuge

71,272 acres, USFWS, (402) 376-1889

Many lakes and marshes amid undulating prairie in the heart of the Sandhills. Observation blinds provided for viewing courtship displays of greater prairie-chickens and sharp-tailed grouse.

Straddles Highway 83, about equidistant (25 miles) from Thedford and Valentine. To visit Hackberry Headquarters, go 13 miles west of Highway 83 on Spur 16B.

9 Samuel R. McKelvie National Forest

115,703 acres, USDA-FS, (402) 823-4154

See-forever upland grasslands. Only 2,500 acres are forested.

From Nenzel, on Highway 20, go south on Spur 16F. After about 16 miles, follow the road east toward Merritt Reservoir. Visitors are advised to tour on paved roadways, as maze of sand tracks through prairie can be confusing and impassable, even in 4WD vehicles.

10 Fort Niobrara National Wildlife Refuge

19,122 acres, USFWS, (402) 376-3789
A 1.5-mile wildlife drive through Sandhills prairie provides intimate views of bison, elk, prairie dogs, and burrowing owls.

From Valentine, go east 4 miles on Highway 12.

11 Niobrara Valley Preserve

65,000 acres, TNC, (402) 722-4440
Two hiking trails wind through Sandhills prairie and woodlands of ponderosa pine, birch, basswood, bur oak, and cottonwood along the Niobrara River.

From Johnstown, on Highway 20, go north about 12 miles on dirt road (toward Norden). Road impassable in wet weather.

12 Lillian Annette Rowe Sanctuary

1,150 acres, NAS, (308) 468-5282
Classic tableau of prairie, wet meadow, and river channel. Observation blinds on Platte River for sandhill crane and waterfowl viewing in March and early April (reservations required).

From I-80, take Exit 285, go south 2 miles, then west 2 miles to 44450 Elm Island Road.

13 Crane Meadows

250 acres, Crane Meadows Nature Center, (308) 382-1820
A swatch of prairie along north channel of Platte River. In March and early April, nature center staff leads tours to sandhill crane–viewing bunker on Mormon Island, a lovely prairie and wet meadow landscape owned by the Platte River Whooping Crane Maintenance Trust.

Nature center headquarters is at Exit 305 on I-80. Crane Meadows is about 1 mile farther south on Alda Road.

14 Platte Prairie and Wetland Corridor

Approximately 4,000 acres in scattered sites, TNC, (402) 694-4191;
Prairie Plains Resource Institute, (402) 694-5535
Mosaic of native prairies, wet meadows, and restored grasslands on
Platte River between Grand Island and Columbus. Excellent example
of restoration and compatible economic development, conducted by
the Nature Conservancy and Prairie Plains Resource Institute. PPRI
conducts annual children's nature camp for third- to sixth-grade stu-
dents called SOAR, Summer Orientation about Rivers.

Call TNC or PPRI for information about field trips and volunteer
opportunities.

15 Rainwater Basin

29,000 acres, Rainwater Basin Joint Venture, (308) 385-6465,
(308) 236-5015, (402) 471-0641
Definitive example of the companionship of wetlands and prairies.
Cooperative efforts among farmers and government agencies to restore
numerous wetlands and mixed-grass prairies within this system.

Basins are scattered across seventeen-county area of south central
Nebraska. A fine cluster of wetlands lies around Clay Center. For
information on sites with public access, contact phone numbers above.

16 Willa Cather Memorial Prairie

610 acres, TNC, (402) 342-0282
Remnant mixed-grass prairie that evokes writings of Cather, who
spent her childhood in nearby Red Cloud, whose "shaggy grass country . . . gripped me with a passion I have never been able to shake."

From Red Cloud, go 5 miles south on Highway 281.

17 Nine-Mile Prairie

230 acres, University of Nebraska at Lincoln, (402) 472-2971
One of very few tracts of tallgrass prairie remaining in eastern
Nebraska. Study site for the research of J. E. Weaver, the father of grassland ecology. Photo of Nine-Mile Prairie, by Michael Forsberg, fea-
tured on seventy-cent U.S. postage stamp issued in 2001.

From I-80, take Highway 34 (Exit 401) northwest 4 miles to NW 48th Street. Go south .8 mile, then west 1 mile on W. Fletcher Avenue.

18 Little Salt Fork Marsh

200 acres, TNC, (402) 342-0282

Restored prairie marsh harboring peculiar saline-tolerant plants as well as the Salt Creek tiger beetle, one of the rarest insects in North America. Last vestige of a network of streams and wetlands in and around city of Lincoln. Much has been destroyed by urban development.

From I-80, go about .5 mile on Highway 34 (Exit 401) to the first signal light. Take N. 1st Street (unpaved road) north 6 miles to W. Raymond Road. Preserve lies in northwest corner of intersection.

19 Audubon Spring Creek Prairie

626 acres, NAS, (402) 797-2301

Tallgrass prairie, wetlands, bur oak woodlands, original wagon ruts from Nebraska City–Fort Kearny cutoff of Oregon Trail.

From Lincoln, go west on Highway 6 (O Street) to Emerald. At flashing light signal, go south 5 miles on Spur 55A (NW 84th Street) to Denton, then west about .5 mile on W. Denton Road, which turns south and becomes SW 98th Street. Continue 3 miles to preserve entrance.

20 Allwine Prairie

160 acres, University of Nebraska at Omaha, (402) 554-3378

Large restored tallgrass prairie on western suburban fringe of Omaha. Encompasses stream, spring-fed seeps, and upland tallgrass prairie. Efforts are under way to expand prairie to create 600-acre Glacier Creek Preserve and Metropolitan Environmental Study Center.

From I-680 in west Omaha, take W. Dodge Road (Exit 3) west to 144th Street. Go north on 144th Street to State Street, then west .5 mile on State Street to preserve entrance, which is marked by sign.

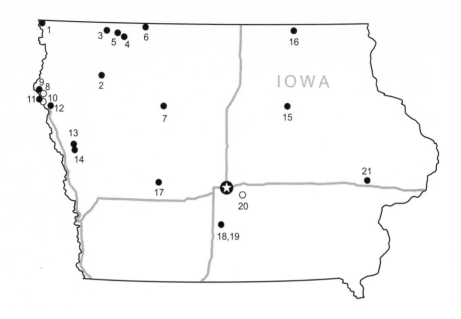

● < 1,000 acres
○ 1,000–10,000 acres

IOWA

Most of Iowa—more than 98 percent—is privately owned and in agricultural production. Hence, little prairie remains, and these remnants are scattered far and wide. Prairies smaller than 100 acres are not noted here, unless for ineffable reasons they are dear to my heart, for which I claim an author's prerogative. For a complete list of the Hawkeye State's prairies, see the *Guide to Iowa's State Preserves* or the Iowa Department of Natural Resources Web site.

Most visitors know Iowa from travels on I-80, which bisects the state east-west. The interstate traverses the Southern Iowa Drift Plain, a soothing landscape of ancient glacial drift that has been shaped by erosion into roly-poly hills. These are the hills Grant Wood depicted so voluptuously in his paintings. To see Iowa's other shapes, a visitor must get off I-80. A tour of prairies will be greatly enhanced with the companionship of Jean Prior's *Landforms of Iowa*. She provides, with words and pictures, a clear explanation of the state's lovely and often subtle shapes. Geologists divide Iowa into eight landform regions, two of which I reference in the prairie list below—the Des Moines Lobe and the Loess Hills—because they provide a logical framework for visiting prairies with similar affinities.

1 Gitchie Manitou State Preserve

91 acres, IDNR, (515) 281-3891
Destination for Iowa botanists and prairie-philes for more than a century. Prairie, woodland, and old fields with outcrops of 1.6-billion-year-old Sioux quartzite, oldest exposed bedrock in Iowa. Also has archaeological sites.

From Larchwood, go west 6.5 miles on County Road A18, then north about 4.5 miles on County Road K10.

2 Steele Prairie State Preserve

200 acres in two tracts, IDNR, Cherokee CCB, (712) 225-6709
Together, the two tracts contain one of the last large remnants of tall-grass prairie in Iowa. Includes sedge meadow and marsh.

Just north of Larrabee, at intersection of Highway 59 and County Road C16, go west 1 mile on C16, turn north on gravel road for .5 mile to 40-acre tract east of road. Continue north about .75 mile, then west .75 mile to the 160-acre tract south of road.

THE DES MOINES LOBE

This landform region in north central Iowa reveals the powerful effects of the most recent glaciation, which occurred 12,000 to 14,000 years ago. It is a "young" landscape, where water is still trying to shape the terrain. On a map of the state, the Des Moines Lobe resembles a tongue lapping into Iowa from North and South Dakota and Minnesota, with its tip terminating along the Raccoon River and the present-day city of Des Moines. Travelers on I-35 north of Des Moines go through the heart of the Des Moines Lobe. The following five sites provide public access.

3 Ocheyedan Mound State Preserve

24 acres, Osceola CCB, (712) 758-3709
A high point of Iowa's glacial past, affording fine vistas of surrounding subtly undulating landscape. The 100-foot pile of sand and gravel is called a kame. Its covering of dry prairie resembles a badly barbered crew cut.

From Ocheyedan, go south about 1.5 miles on County Road L58, then east 1 mile on County Road A22.

4 Freda Haffner Kettlehole State Preserve

110 acres, TNC, (515) 244-5044
Glacial landscape of prairies and wetlands. The large kettlehole near the middle of the preserve was formed when gravel deposits settled around a large block of ice as it melted during the last glacial advance in the area.

North of Milford, go about 1 mile north on U.S. 71, then west about 1.5 mile on Highway 86. Where Highway 86 turns north, continue *west* on 210th Street (gravel) for about 2 miles to preserve on north side of road.

5 Cayler Prairie State Preserve

160 acres, IDNR, (515) 281-3891

Superb array of plant communities resulting from complex landform left in wake of most recent glaciation.

From Spirit Lake, go west about 9.5 miles on Highway 9, then south 2.5 miles on County Road M38 (170th Avenue, gravel) to preserve on east side of road.

6 Anderson Prairie State Preserve

200 acres, IDNR, (515) 281-3891

Glacial landscape of tallgrass prairie, wetlands, oak savanna, floodplain woods.

From Estherville, go west about 2.5 miles on Highway 9 to gravel road opposite County Road N25. Go north on gravel road 1.5 miles to preserve on east side of road.

7 Kalsow Prairie State Preserve

160 acres, IDNR, (515) 281-3891

Tallgrass prairie and pothole wetlands. A classic Des Moines Lobe site that demonstrates how water on a "young" landscape is still struggling to carve an escape route. Can be squishy during wet springs.

From southern edge of Manson, at intersection of Highway 7 and County Road N65, go north 4 miles on County Road N65, then west 1 mile to preserve on south side of road.

THE LOESS HILLS

The Loess Hills look a great deal like a gigantic spinal column lying along Iowa's western border with the Missouri River. The 200-mile-long ridge, which extends about 40 miles into northwestern Missouri, is composed of soil called loess, fine quartz silt picked up from glacial floodplains and redeposited elsewhere by prevailing winds. Loess soils are common throughout the prairie states, but nowhere in North America has loess piled up as deep and dramatically as in the Loess Hills of Iowa. Loess soils are extremely fertile; however, the Loess Hills proved too rugged to cultivate extensively. For this reason, the largest undisturbed prairie remnants in Iowa are found amid these craggy hills. The major threats to the remaining prairies are the encroachment of trees and woody vegetation, caused by a century's lack of fire, and the invasion of suburbanites building homes with scenic views from the ridge tops. The Loess Hills Scenic Byway is a 220-mile-long route through this amazing landform. For byway maps and information, contact the Loess Hills Scenic Byway Council, (712) 482-3029, or www.byways.org. The following seven sites provide public access.

8 Broken Kettle Grasslands

3,000 acres, TNC, (515) 244-5044

Tallgrass prairie on steep, crumpled ridges mingles with bur oak woodlands. Spectacular vistas. Broken Kettle, with neighboring Five Ridge Prairie State Preserve, forms by far the largest prairie landscape in Iowa.

From I-29 in Sioux City, take Highway 12 (Exit 151) north about 10 miles to intersection with County Road K18. Continue on Highway 12 another 4 miles to Butcher Road, then east about 1 mile on Butcher Road.

9 Five Ridge Prairie State Preserve

789 acres, TNC, Plymouth CCB, (712) 947-4270

Preserve is named for five prominent ridges, which are covered with tallgrass prairie on their south- and west-facing slopes. Bur oak woodlands nestle in the valleys, while invasive dogwood thickets clamber up and over the slopes into the prairie. More great views.

From I-29 in Sioux City, take Highway 12 (Exit 151) north about 10 miles to County Road K18. Go northeast about 3 miles on K18, then west on 260th Avenue (gravel) 1 mile to preserve entrance. This gravel road is about .5 mile south of County Road C43.

10 Stone State Park

1,069 acres, IDNR, (712) 255-4698
Combines rugged beauty of Loess Hills with amenities, such as picnic tables and public restrooms, seldom encountered in wilder prairie settings. Variety of designated-use trails.

From I-29 in Sioux City, take Highway 12 (Exit 151) 4 miles to park's west entrance.

11 Mount Talbot State Preserve

90 acres, IDNR, (515) 281-3891
Tallgrass prairie on dramatic Loess Hill ridges. Prime butterfly habitat.

Follow directions to Stone State Park above. Preserve is accessible from within park or from Rock River Road, which forms park's northern boundary.

12 Sioux City Prairie

157 acres, TNC, (515) 244-5044
Tallgrass prairie meets city. Said to be one of the largest native prairies in urban setting in U.S.

From I-29 in Sioux City, take Hamilton Boulevard (Exit 149) through town to Stone Park Boulevard. Go northwest on Stone Park Boulevard to Clifton Avenue. Go left onto Clifton Avenue, then left on Rebecca Street, then right on College Road. The prairie is east of Briar Cliff University campus. Park in west campus lot.

13 Sylvan Runkel State Preserve

330 acres, IDNR, (515) 281-3891
Tallgrass prairie on rugged ridge, within 2,742-acre Loess Hills Wildlife Management Area. Preserve named for longtime Iowa naturalist and champion of the Loess Hills.

East of Onawa, at intersection of Highway 175 and County Road L12, take L12 north 6.8 miles, cross two levees, turn east on Nutmeg Avenue (gravel), cross bridge over Little Sioux River. Immediately east of bridge, turn south on 178th Street (gravel, winding) and go about 2 miles to Oak Avenue. Preserve entrance just north of this intersection.

14 Turin Loess Hills State Preserve

220 acres, IDNR, (515) 281-3891

Ridge top tallgrass prairies. A National Natural Landmark.

From Turin, go north 1.5 miles on Larpenteur Memorial Road (gravel) to parking area on east side of road.

15 Cedar Hills Sand Prairie State Preserve

90 acres, TNC, (515) 244-5044

Diverse landscape in small space, including wet prairie, sand prairie, and fen amid sand dunes.

On northern edge of Cedar Falls, at intersection of Hudson Road and Highway 57, go west about 1.5 miles on Highway 57, north about 2.5 miles on County Road T75, west about 2.5 miles on County Road C67, then north 1.5 miles on Butler Avenue (gravel). Preserve is on east side of road.

16 Hayden Prairie State Preserve

240 acres, IDNR, (515) 281-3891

Largest blacksoil prairie remnant in Iowa with impressive wildflower diversity. Commemorates Ada Hayden, botanist and early proponent of prairie preservation in Iowa.

From Chester, go south 3 miles on County Road V26, then west 1 mile on County Road A23.

17 Sheeder Prairie State Preserve

25 acres, IDNR, (515) 281-3891

Tiny prairie with three assets: great introduction to the topography of the Southern Iowa Drift Plain, which water has eroded into roller coaster hills since the last period of glaciation 500,000 years ago; fine wildflower displays in midsummer; and reasonable access from I-80.

From I-80, take Casey exit (83), go east about 2 miles on Highway 925, north about 11 miles on Highway 25 to Guthrie Center, west about 4 miles on Highway 44, north 1 mile on Indigo Road (gravel) to T intersection with 220th Street, then east .25 mile to preserve on north side of road.

18 Rolling Thunder Prairie State Preserve

123 acres, Warren CCB, (515) 961-6169
Dry tallgrass prairies on ridge tops, mesic prairies on slopes, woodlands along creek.

From Indianola at intersection of Highway 65/69 and Highway 92, go south on Highway 69 for 12 miles to County Road G76. Turn west, go 3 miles to County Road R57, then .75 mile north to preserve on west side of road.

19 Medora Prairie

100 acres, TNC, (515) 244-5044
About 60 acres of tallgrass prairie interlaced with wooded ravines. With nearby Rolling Thunder, embraces some of the last virgin tallgrass in southern Iowa.

From intersection of Highway 69 and County Road G76 south of Indianola, go west about 2 miles on County Road G76, then north 1 mile on 90th Avenue to Tyler Street.

20 Neal Smith National Wildlife Refuge

5,065 acres, USFWS, (515) 994-3400
An idea whose time has come. Refuge was established in 1991 (as Walnut Creek National Wildlife Refuge) with purpose of remaking a representative piece of the tallgrass—oak savanna landscape that formerly cloaked the rolling hills of southern Iowa. The goal is to reestablish 8,600 acres of vegetation and bring back the prairie tenants—bison were reintroduced in 1996 and elk in 1998. The largest reconstruction project within the historic range of tallgrass prairie. Prairie Learning Center, nature trails, and auto tour route.

From I-80, take Colfax exit (155), go south 7 miles on Highway 117 to Prairie City. Continue on Highway 117 through Prairie City, across the Highway 163 bridge, to refuge entrance.

21 Rochester Cemetery Prairie

10 acres, Rochester Township, Cedar CCB, (563) 886-6930
Exquisite old cemetery where tombstones are shaded by giant bur oaks. A classic expression of tallgrass prairie—bur oak savanna lying

on sandy terrain near the Cedar River. Well known for display of shooting stars (a wildflower) in late May. Visit with requisite reverence for the dead and do not pick flowers or harvest prairie seed.

On I-80, about 13 miles east of Iowa City, take Tipton exit (267), go north 1.6 miles on Highway 38 to Cemetery Road, then west .3 mile to cemetery on either side of gravel road.

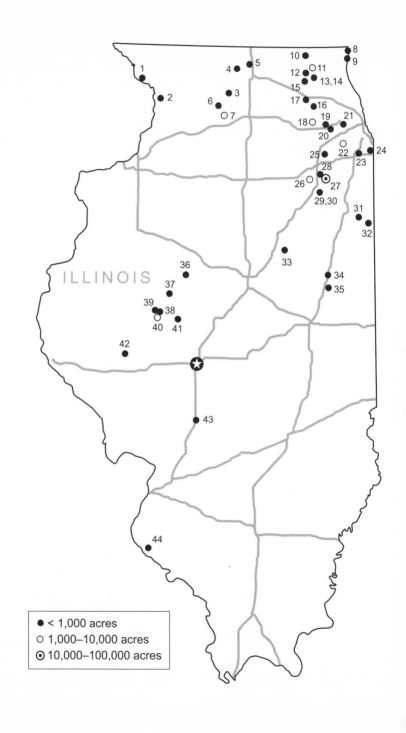

ILLINOIS

Illinois lies in the heart of the Prairie Peninsula, the glacial plain rolling in oceanic swells from northeastern Missouri to Ohio. Tidily and quickly converted to pasture and crops by European settlers, it used to be a vast mosaic of tallgrass prairie, savanna, and forest. So little remains of the natural fabric of Illinois that it is easy for a fainthearted person to slip into despair. I will never forget the sinking feeling that I had standing out on 5-acre Weston Cemetery Prairie at sunset, with black thunderclouds rolling in from the west, knowing that I was standing on one of the last unplowed fragments of the Grand Prairie, a landscape of black-soil tallgrass that once encompassed 13 million acres of Illinois.

What is fascinating about the paucity of natural landscapes in Illinois is the determination of the conservation community—especially within metropolitan Chicago—to protect what is left and restore what has been altered. Their level of energy, commitment, and optimism, which seems to be in inverse relation to the amount of prairie remaining, is quite inspiring. One example of this stamina, which occurred in 1990, involved the salvage of a native prairie on land that was being mined for gravel. Over the course of two days, several hundred volunteers, using bulldozers, dump trucks, and bare hands, scraped up the prairie as best they could and transplanted it with some success to a gravelly hill at Bluff Spring Fen.

NORTHWESTERN ILLINOIS

1 Hanover Bluff Nature Preserve
362 acres, IDNR, (815) 885-2204, (217) 785-8686
High dolomite ridge overlooking the Mississippi River, includes sand-hill prairie, seep springs, and upland forest. The first dedicated Nature Preserve in the Wisconsin Driftless Natural Division.

From Hanover, take Hanover Hill Road southeast 1.5 miles, then go south .25 mile on Whitton Road. Preserve is on bluffs east of road.

2 Ayers Sand Prairie Nature Preserve

109 acres, IDNR, (815) 885-2204, (217) 785-8686

Sand prairie, sand dunes, and areas of actively moving sand called blowouts. Inhabited by a number of the reptiles found in sand prairies.

From Savanna, go south 2.7 miles on Highway 84, then east .5 mile on Airport Road. Preserve is north of road.

3 Jarrett Prairie Nature Preserve

116 acres, Byron Forest Preserve District, (815) 234-8535

Dry prairie remnant on thin-soiled dolomite ridges with mesic prairie in swales. Prairie trail maps available at Jarrett Prairie Center.

From Byron, cross the Rock River on Highway 72, then go .5 mile west on River Road to entrance of forest preserve.

4 Searls Park Prairie Nature Preserve

66 acres, Rockford Park District, (815) 987-8800

Largest remaining vestige of blacksoil prairie in northwestern Illinois.

In west Rockford, at intersection of Business Highway 20 (W. State Street) and Central Avenue, go north 1.8 miles on Central Avenue to Searls Memorial Park.

5 Harlem Hills Prairie Nature Preserve

53 acres, IDNR, (815) 885-2204, (217) 785-8686

Considered to be the finest remaining gravel hill prairie in Illinois. Notable wildflower diversity.

In north Rockford, on north side of Loves Park, at intersection of Highway 251 and Windsor Road, go east 1.3 miles on Windsor Road to T intersection, then north .1 mile on Forest Hills Road, then east .1 mile on Flora Drive. Preserve is on south side of road.

6 George B. Fell Nature Preserve

685 acres, IDNR, (815) 732-6185

Diverse assemblage of upland and floodplain forest, sandstone cliffs, relict boreal vegetation, and prairie within Castle Rock State Park on scenic Rock River. Named for indefatigable conservationist and founder of Illinois' nature preserve system.

From Oregon, at intersection of Highway 2 and Highway 64, go south and west 4 miles on Highway 2 to park entrance.

7 Nachusa Grasslands

1,500 acres, TNC, (815) 456-2340

Splendid vistas on one of best remaining prairiescapes in Illinois. Encompasses dry prairie, tallgrass prairie, bur oak savanna, fen, and marsh amid sandstone outcrops. Management includes restoration of old fields interspersed with high-quality prairie. Open for hiking and birdwatching.

In Franklin Grove, go north 1.5 miles on Daysville Road (1700 East) to Naylor Road (1950 North), then west 2.2 miles to Lowden Road (1500 East). Turn north and go 1 mile. Entrance is on west side of road.

METRO CHICAGO

8 North Dunes Nature Preserve

200 acres, IDNR, (867) 662-4828

Continuation of prairie-dune landscape within Illinois Beach Nature Preserve (see below).

From Zion, go north on Sheridan Road (Highway 137) to 17th Street, then east about 1 mile on 17th Street through north unit of Illinois Beach State Park. Preserve is on south side of road.

9 Illinois Beach Nature Preserve

829 acres, IDNR, (847) 662-4828

Exquisite dune and swale topography within Illinois Beach State Park on shore of Lake Michigan; numerous prairie and wetland communities support high diversity of plants and animals. First Illinois Nature Preserve, dedicated in 1964. A National Natural Landmark.

From Zion, take Sheridan Road (Highway 137) south 1 mile, then go east on Wadsworth Road to park entrance. Nature preserve is south of park lodge.

10 Glacial Park Nature Preserve

330 acres, MCCD, (815) 338-6223
Great glacial mishmash of tallgrass prairie, oak savanna, dry hill prairie,
kettle bogs, fen, and sedge meadow. Lies along Nippersink Creek, one of
Illinois' highest-quality streams. Preserve is within 2,600-acre Glacial
Park, which includes the rail-to-trail Prairie Trail.

In McHenry, at intersection of Highway 120 and Highway 31
(Richmond Road), go north about 6.5 miles on Highway 31, then west
.6 mile on Harts Road to park entrance.

11 Moraine Hills State Park

1,690 acres, IDNR, (815) 385-1624
Undulating glacial features very prominent in this large park in the
Fox River Valley. Leatherleaf Bog is an excellent example of kettle-
moraine topography.

From just west of Wauconda, at intersection of Highway 12 and
Highway 176, go northwest about 4.5 miles on Highway 176, then north
2 miles on River Road to park entrance.

12 Wingate Prairie Nature Preserve

39 acres, Crystal Lake Park District, (815) 459-0680
Dry-mesic gravel prairie, extremely rare in Illinois. Named for Bill
Wingate, teacher and prairie enthusiast who spearheaded restoration
of site.

In Crystal Lake, just north of intersection of Terra Cotta Avenue
(Highway 176) and Main Street within Veteran Acres Park.

13 Lyons Prairie and Marsh Nature Preserve

300 acres, MCCD, (815) 338-6223
Actively restored wet prairie and marsh in glacial outwash along Fox
River. Floating boardwalk across sedge meadow. Recent reports in
Chicago Wilderness Magazine note late summer tallgrass reaching
heights of 8 feet.

From southeast of Crystal Lake, at intersection of Highway 14 and
Highway 31, go southeast 1.4 miles on Highway 14, east 3 miles on Three

Oaks Road, then north .8 mile on County Line Road. Preserve is east of road.

14 Fel-Pro RRR Preserve

220 acres, TNC, (312) 580-2100
Gravel hill prairie, savanna, sedge meadow, fen, and spring-fed lakes in Fox River Valley. Restoration work in progress. Former retreat for employees of Fel-Pro, manufacturer of automobile gaskets well known for its progressive policies, including on-site child care, in-home caregiving, and summer day camp. The triple R is part of Fel-Pro's original name for the park, which stands for rest, relaxation, and recreation. Call TNC for information about hours, which vary seasonally.

In Cary, at intersection of Highway 14 and Silver Lake Road, go north about 1.5 miles on Silver Lake Road until it dead-ends at Crystal Lake Avenue. Go east about 1 mile on Crystal Lake Avenue. After the road curves south, look for small road to the east, which is entrance to preserve.

15 Lake-in-the-Hills Fen Nature Preserve

400 acres, MCCD, (815) 678-4431
Gorgeous glacial landscape includes dry hill prairie, sedge meadow, and hanging fens as well as the state's smallest dragonfly.

In Algonquin, at intersection of Highway 31 and Highway 62 (Algonquin Road), go west 1 mile on Highway 62, then north 1.3 miles on Pyott Road to Barbara Key Park. Turn left into park and follow road to parking lot in rear.

16 Bluff Spring Fen

91 acres, TNC, (312) 580-2100; Friends of the Fen, (847) 464-4426
Rolling glacial landscape of dry hill prairie, blacksoil prairie, sedge meadow, fen, and oak-hickory savanna in Bluff City Cemetery on southeast edge of Elgin. Remarkable reclamation story. Prior to 1979, when restoration began, site was a gravel quarry, illegal dump, and track for off-road vehicles. Now trails are for hiking and birding; maps and trail guides available at kiosk.

Take Highway 20 (Lake Street) to east side of Elgin, go south on Bluff City Boulevard (stoplight also marked Shales Parkway) to cemetery. Take road in cemetery to southwest corner parking lot with split rail fence.

17 Horlock Hill Prairie State Preserve/LeRoy Oakes Forest Preserve

264 acres, Kane County Forest Preserve District, (847) 741-9798

Formerly a farm, now a blend of woodlands and prairie, including a dry hill prairie that has been a high school restoration project led by science teacher Bob Horlock for more than thirty years.

From I-90, just west of Elgin, take Randall Road exit, go south to Dean Street, then west about .75 mile on Dean Street. Prairie areas are on south side of road.

18 Fermilab Prairie

1,100 acres, U.S. Department of Energy, (630) 840-3303, (630) 840-5588

Where particle physics meets the prairie. Ongoing prairie restoration efforts began in 1975 on land atop the accelerator. Portions of prairie are open to public with trails and interpretive signs, and Fermilab leads seasonal tours.

From I-88/Farnsworth Avenue tollway interchange, go 3 miles north on Kirk Avenue, then take Pine Street to west entrance of Fermilab.

19 Schulenberg Prairie

100 acres, Morton Arboretum, (630) 968-0074

This prairie and oak savanna was planted by, and named for, Morton staff horticulturist and prairie ecologist Ray Schulenberg. Begun in 1962, it has served as a template for other prairie restorations in the Chicago area. At west end of arboretum.

From Chicago, go west on I-88 to Lisle, take Highway 53 exit north about .5 mile. Arboretum is on west side of road and clearly marked with signs.

20 Belmont Prairie Nature Preserve

25 acres, Downers Grove Park District, (630) 963-1304

Small but rich pocket of dry and mesic prairies and marshy areas on slope of Valparaiso Moraine. Notable wildflower diversity. Actively being restored.

In Downers Grove, at intersection of Highway 34 (Ogden Avenue) and Belmont Road, go south .6 mile on Belmont Road, west .5 mile on Haddow Avenue, then north on Cross Street to preserve parking lot. Preserve is west of Downers Grove Golf Course.

21 Wolf Road Prairie

80 acres, Save the Prairie Society, (708) 865-8736

Prairie's Last Stand. This unbelievable parcel of tallgrass prairie and oak savanna in metro Chicago is *the* metaphor for the perpetual standoff between land conservationists and urban developers. Efforts to protect the site began in 1975. Prairie has high wildflower diversity.

From I-294 (Tri-State Tollway), go east .75 mile on Highway 34 (Ogden Avenue), then north 1 mile on Wolf Road to 31st Street. Preserve is north of 31st Street and west of Wolf Road.

22 Cap Sauers Holding Nature Preserve

1,670 acres, CCFPD, (708) 771-1330

Degraded prairie and oak savanna are being restored within the largest nature preserve in northeastern Illinois. Site is notable for impressive glacial features (it lies on Valparaiso Moraine) and its location along Des Plaines River. Call CCFPD for information on location of prairie areas within the preserve.

At intersection of Highway 12/20 and Highway 45, west of Hickory Hills, go south 5.5 miles on Highway 45, then west 1.5 miles on McCarthy Road. Preserve is bounded on north by Calumet Sag Road and on east by 104th Avenue.

23 Indian Boundary Prairies

Approximately 300 acres in scattered sites, multiple ownership, contact TNC, (312) 580-2100

100-acre Gensburg-Markham Prairie, 12-acre Dropseed Prairie, 60-acre Paintbrush Prairie, and 80-acre Sundrop Prairie form an archipelago of remnant grasslands known collectively as the Indian Boundary Prairies. The cluster is one of the best remaining grasslands in Illinois. Name derives from boundary established by 1795 treaty whereby Potawatomi relinquished land east of the line to U.S. The prairies are owned and managed by TNC, Northeastern Illinois University, and the Natural Land Institute, with Friends of the Indian Boundary Prairies providing volunteer stewardship. A National Natural Landmark, the prairies are in the city of Markham, which dubs itself the Prairie Capital of the Prairie State.

Gensburg-Markham Prairie: From I-57 (Dan Ryan Expressway), take 159th Street exit (Highway 6) east to Whipple Avenue, then go north on Whipple to parking lot for prairie. Dropseed Prairie: From I-57, take 159th Street exit east to Kedzie Avenue (first major signal light), go north on Kedzie, west on 157th Street, then north on Homan Avenue one block; prairie is on west side of road. Paintbrush Prairie: From I-57, take 159th Street exit west to Pulaski Road, go north on Pulaski, east on 155th Street, then north on Millard Avenue to end of road. Sundrop Prairie: From I-57, take 159th Street exit east to Kedzie Avenue (first major signal light), then go north on Kedzie; prairie is on west side of road.

24 Sand Ridge Nature Preserve

70 acres, CCFPD, Sand Ridge Nature Center, (708) 868-0606
Dunes and swales formed by ebbing Lake Michigan. Sand prairie and black oak savanna on ridges alternate with marshy habitats in clay-based swales. Access by prior permission only.

From I-94, in South Holland, take 159th Street exit east 1 mile, go north 1 mile on Torrence Avenue (Highway 83), then east .4 mile on 154th Street. Preserve is south of road.

25 Lockport Prairie Nature Preserve

254 acres, Metropolitan Water Reclamation District of Greater Chicago, WCFPD, (815) 727-8700
Exposed bedrock supporting rare dolomite prairie plus fens, marshes, and dry prairie ridges in Des Plaines River Valley. Home to the endangered leafy prairie clover and the rare prairie satin grass.

From I-55 (Stevenson Expressway) in Lockport, take Highway 53 exit south about 7.5 miles, turn east on Division Street and go .2 mile down steep slope of glacial outwash to flats. Prairie is on both sides of road from the railroad tracks to the Des Plaines River.

26 Goose Lake Prairie State Park

2,537 acres, IDNR, (815) 942-2899

A crown jewel of Chicago-area natural landscapes and the largest remnant tallgrass prairie in Illinois. Prairie intermingles with marsh near confluence of Kankakee, Des Plaines, and Illinois Rivers. Goose Lake Prairie provides a glimpse of what nearby Midewin tallgrass restoration project (see next entry below) might someday resemble on a larger scale. Excellent trails and interpretive programs. Flurry of industrial activity in the vicinity, including a power generation facility, can make a visit to this prairie seem somewhat surreal.

From Morris, take Highway 47 south across Illinois River, continue for .7 mile, go east 6 miles on Pine Bluff Road, then north on Jugtown Road to park entrance.

27 Midewin National Tallgrass Prairie

15,080 acres, USDA-FS, (815) 423-6370

Guns to grass! A remarkable tallgrass prairie restoration effort is occurring on the former site of the Joliet Army Ammunition Plant. Midewin (Potawatomi for healing society) will form the centerpiece of the 40,000-acre Prairie Parklands Macrosite, a public-private initiative to "heal" and protect natural areas at the confluence of the Des Plaines, Kankakee, and Illinois Rivers. Landscape also encompasses upland forest, oak savanna, wetlands, and rare examples of dolomite prairies.

From I-55, take Arsenal Road exit (245), go east on Arsenal Road for 6 miles to the intersection of Highway 53, then south on Highway 53 for 6.8 miles to the supervisor's office on east side of highway. Contact the Midewin Administrative Center, 30071 S. State Highway 53 in Wilmington, for information on tours and trails.

28 Grant Creek Prairie Nature Preserve

78 acres, IDNR, (815) 423-5326

High-quality remnants of wet, mesic, and dolomite prairies in a somewhat inaccessible location within Des Plaines Fish and Wildlife Area.

From I-55, take Wilmington exit (241), then take east frontage road of I-55 north for .8 mile. Frontage road dead-ends at south end of preserve. Frontage road is rough.

29 Braidwood Dunes and Savanna Nature Preserve

298 acres, WCFPD, *(815) 727-8700*

Sand prairie and savanna, sedge meadow, and marsh. Impressive remnant of landscape formed 13,000 years ago by glacial deposits dropped during Kankakee Torrent.

From Braidwood, at intersection of Highway 53 and Highway 113, take Highway 113 southeast .8 mile. Preserve entrance is on south side of road.

30 Wilmington Shrub Prairie Nature Preserve

146 acres, IDNR, *(217) 785-8686*

With resemblances to Braidwood Dunes, includes rare shrub prairie, sand prairie and savanna, sedge meadow, and marsh.

From Braidwood, at intersection of Highway 53 and Highway 113, take Highway 113 east 3 miles, then go north 1.5 miles on county road that parallels Kankakee River. Take footpath .5 mile to preserve on west side of road.

31 Kankakee Sands Preserve

650 acres, TNC, *(312) 580-2100*

Oak barrens, sedge meadows, and prairie amid sand dunes. Preserve is part of larger bistate effort to restore the path of oak savanna that once straddled Illinois and Indiana.

In St. Anne Township. Contact TNC regarding access.

32 Hooper Branch Savanna Nature Preserve

483 acres, IDNR, *(217) 785-8686*

Best public access onto exquisitely peculiar landscapes of the Kankakee Sands. Sand savanna amid impressive dunes and swales formed during the Kankakee Torrent, a huge flood that occurred during a period of glacial melting 15,000 years ago. Some dunes reach heights of almost 700 feet. Located within Iroquois County State Wildlife Area.

From St. Anne, take Highway 1 south 2 miles, then go east 9 miles. Preserve is northwest of parking lot in wildlife area.

THE GRAND PRAIRIE

The following three cemetery prairie nature preserves form a poignant triad. Each is a tiny patch of blacksoil tallgrass prairie representative of the Grand Prairie, which formerly covered 13 million acres of central Illinois.

33 Weston Cemetery Prairie

5 acres, Yates Township and ParkLands Foundation, (309) 454-3169
From I-55, take Highway 24 (Exit 187) east 6.5 miles, then take lane north .3 mile to cemetery parking lot.

34 Loda Cemetery Prairie Nature Preserve

3.4 acres, TNC, (312) 580-2100
From center of Loda, take road west .3 mile, then go north .6 mile. Preserve lies north of cemetery.

35 Prospect Cemetery Prairie Nature Preserve

5 acres, Paxton Township Cemetery Association, (217) 379-2676
In Paxton, at intersection of Highway 9 and Highway 45, take Highway 45 south 1 mile to Green Street, then turn east .2 mile. Preserve lies to the east.

THE ILLINOIS RIVER

36 Manito Prairie Nature Preserve

20 acres, IDNR, (217) 785-8686
Gravel hill and sand prairies on terrace above Illinois River.
From Manito, take blacktop road heading north out of town for 7.5 miles to where road turns east. Preserve is north of road.

37 Henry Allan Gleason Nature Preserve

110 acres, IDNR, (217) 785-8686

Sand prairie, sand dunes—including a 60-foot stabilized dune—and blowouts on Illinois River. Named for distinguished plant ecologist and coauthor of *The Natural Geography of Plants*. Located in southwest corner of Sand Ridge State Forest.

From Topeka, take road heading north out of town for 1 mile, jog east .2 mile, then continue north 2 miles. Preserve is .2 mile west of road. There are no trails.

38 Long Branch Sand Prairie Nature Preserve

93 acres, IDNR, (217) 785-8686

Sand prairie on gently rolling dunes.

From Kilbourne, go north 4 miles on Highway 97, west 2 miles on county road, then north .5 mile on county road. Preserve is west of road.

39 Matanzas Prairie Nature Preserve

27 acres, IDNR, (217) 785-8686

Rare remaining example of wet sand prairie.

From Bath, go north 1.5 miles on Highway 78, then east .3 mile on blacktop road. Preserve is south of road.

40 Sand Prairie—Scrub Oak Nature Preserve

1,460 acres, IDNR, (217) 785-8686

Beautiful expanse of sand prairie, savanna, and scrubby oak-hickory forest.

From Bath, take road heading east out of town for 3.6 miles, then go south 1.3 miles. Preserve is west of road.

41 Revis Hill Prairie Nature Preserve

53 acres, IDNR, (217) 785-8686

Fine example of loess hill prairie on bluffs above Sangamon River.

From Kilbourne, go north .5 mile on Highway 97, then east 7.5 miles on blacktop road, then south 1 mile on gravel road. Preserve is on northeast side of road.

42 Meredosia Hill Prairie Nature Preserve

30 acres, IDNR, (217) 785-8686
Steep loess hill prairie. Name comes from *marais d'osier*, French for willow swamp.

From Meredosia, go east 2.5 miles on Highway 104, then north .7 mile on Highway 67/100. Take blacktop road east and north 2.5 miles. Preserve is south of road.

43 Roberts Cemetery Savanna Nature Preserve

1.7 acres, Montgomery County Board, Illinois Nature Preserves Commission, (217) 785-8686
Virtually all that remains of the mesic savanna landscape once typical of this region of Illinois. Protected since the cemetery's first burial in 1807.

From Litchfield, go north about 7 miles on I-55 and take Highway 108 exit (60). Go south 1.5 miles on eastern frontage road, then east 2 miles on County Road 1750 North (Honey Bend) to T intersection. Go south .25 mile on County Road 500 East, then turn east at first side road. Follow this road until it curves. Preserve is on east side of road.

44 Fults Hill Prairie Nature Preserve

532 acres, IDNR, (217) 785-8686
Largest remaining undisturbed loess hill prairie along Mississippi River in Illinois. Also upland forest, limestone glade, and sinkhole ponds. Preserve is rugged and remote. A National Natural Landmark.

From village of Fults, go 1.6 miles southeast on Bluff Road. Preserve is northeast of road.

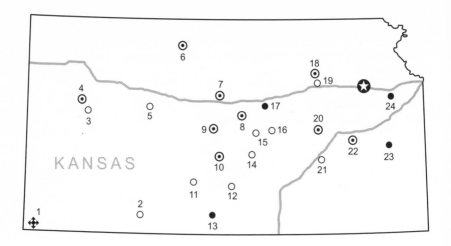

● < 1,000 acres
○ 1,000–10,000 acres
◉ 10,000–100,000 acres
✛ > 100,000 acres

KANSAS

Kansas is very sedimentary. Its deep history involves eons of deposition by oceans and rivers. The geologist Rex Buchanan describes the landforms that comprise Kansas as being, at one time or another, "a shallow sea, a dismal swamp, or a vast salt plain." The resulting stratifications of limestone, shale, and sandstone have created a contemporary landscape that is soothing and majestic.

Dramatic outcrops resembling prows of ocean liners occur throughout the state. One of my favorites is Point of Rocks in Cimarron National Grassland in extreme southwestern Kansas. In western Kansas, along the Smoky Hill River, immense chalk formations stand against the horizon like eroding Egyptian sphinxes. In east central Kansas, the Flint Hills repose like a sleeping giant across the entire breadth of the state. It is here, where the cherty soils were too difficult to plow, that the last unfragmented tallgrass prairies in North America remain. Consequently, the back roads and byways of the Flint Hills are highly recommended, if not obligatory, for prairie seekers, and a companion text for travelers to this part of Kansas would be William Least Heat-Moon's *PrairyErth (A Deep Map)*, an exhaustive history of and tribute to the Flint Hills.

1 Cimarron National Grassland

108,175 acres, USDA-FS, *(620) 697-4621*
Grassland in southwest corner of Kansas hard hit by drought and depression during 1930s Dust Bowl era. Point of Rocks, a limestone promontory overlooking Cimarron River, affords spectacular views. Sandsage prairie is dominant vegetation south of river, while shortgrass prairie predominates to the north. Public access to 23 miles of Santa Fe Trail.

The grassland straddles Highway 27 about 5 miles north of Elkhart. Obtain map and information at ranger station, 242 Highway 56 East in Elkhart.

2 Big Basin Prairie Preserve

1,818 acres, KDWP, (620) 369-2384

Dissolution of massive underground gypsum and salt beds formed sinkhole 1 mile in diameter and 100 feet deep. Short-grass and mixed-grass prairie with bison herd. Fine vistas from basin rim. A National Natural Landmark.

From Minneola, go about 16 miles south on Highway 283 to entrance gate on east side of road.

3 Lake Scott State Park

1,120 acres, KDWP, (620) 872-2061

Large perennial springs burbling up from base of Ogallala aquifer create oasis amid short-grass prairie. Camping, fishing, horseback riding, hiking, wildlife viewing are options.

From Scott City, go north 10 miles on Highway 83 to Highway 95 cutoff; continue north 3 miles on Highway 95 to park entrance.

4 Smoky Valley Ranch

16,800 acres, TNC, (785) 233-4400

Working ranch on Smoky Hill River that sustains a large expanse of mixed-grass prairie.

Located in Logan County. Contact TNC for field trip information.

5 Cedar Bluff State Park and Wildlife Area

9,000 acres, KDWP, (785) 726-3212

Mixed-grass prairie in area of intensive wheat production. Wildlife area is at western end of reservoir. Year-round camping (cabins available) and hiking in park and wildlife area, boating and fishing on 6,000-acre lake.

From Hays, take I-70 west 25 miles, then take Exit 135 onto Highway 147 south 13 miles.

6 Kirwin National Wildlife Refuge

10,778 acres, USFWS, (785) 543-6673

Refuge includes about 4,000 acres of mixed-grass prairie that supports a prairie dog town.

From Glade, go east 6 miles on Highway 9, then south 1 mile.

7 Wilson Reservoir, State Park, and Wildlife Area

18,986 acres, USACE, *(913) 658-2551;* KDWP, *(785) 658-2465*

Sprawling recreational area. As is typical of many Kansas public outdoor places, the focal point is a huge reservoir. Mixed-grass prairie areas include Dakota Trail along Hell Creek and Bur Oak Trail in Sylvan Park. Rocktown Natural Area in Lucas Park combines prairie with gorgeous eroded sandstone formations. Southshore Drive, from state park to Bunker Hill, traverses dramatic sandstone landscape.

From I-70 near Wilson, take Exit 206 north 8 miles to USACE information center below dam; state park office is south of dam.

8 Kanopolis Reservoir and State Park

18,000 acres, USACE, *(785) 546-2294;* KDWP, *(785) 546-2565*

Large areas of mixed-grass prairie surround reservoir; Horsethief Canyon area, in state park, is especially interesting.

From Salina, go 21 miles west on Highway 140, then 9 miles south on Highway 141 to state park office north of dam; USACE information center is on south side of dam.

9 Cheyenne Bottoms

20,000 acres, KDWP, *(620) 793-7730; 7,269 acres,* TNC,
(785) 233-4400

Elliptical 60-square-mile basin containing a prairie marshland teeming with migratory shorebirds and waterfowl in spring, with lesser but still impressive numbers at any one time in fall. One of the finest wetlands in the world.

From Great Bend, take Highway 156 northeast 6 miles to south entrance, or take U.S. 281 north 6 miles to west entrance.

10 Quivira National Wildlife Refuge

22,135 acres, USFWS, *(620) 486-2393*

Salt marshes and sand prairies amid Great Bend Dune Tract of Arkansas River. With Cheyenne Bottoms, forms a significant wetland complex on the Central Flyway.

From Stafford, go east 6 miles on Highway 50 to Zenith, turn north and go 8 miles to the refuge headquarters. From Great Bend, take Highway 281 south to 70th Street, then go east 13 miles.

11 Pratt Sandhills Wildlife Area

4,000 acres, KDWP, (620) 672-5911
Gently undulating sand prairie bisected by only one road.

From Cullison, take Highway 54 west 5 miles, then north 7 miles on sand road.

12 Byron Walker Wildlife Area

4,530 acres, KDWP, (620) 532-3242
Woodlands, wetlands, and sand prairie along South Fork of Ninnescah River.

From Kingman, take Highway 54 west 7 miles.

13 Gypsum Hills Scenic Drive

Land in private ownership
Mixed-grass prairie amid rugged and colorful butte-and-mesa landscape of the Red Hills.

From Medicine Lodge, go west 3.5 miles on Highway 160 and follow 20-mile Gypsum Hills Scenic Drive. Unpaved roads impassable in wet weather.

14 Sand Hills State Park

1,123 acres, KDWP, (620) 542-3664
Beautiful dune and sand prairie landscape with numerous trails.

In Hutchinson, from intersection of Highway 61 and 30th Street, go north 2.3 miles, then east .3 mile on 56th Street to parking lot.

15 McPherson Valley Wetlands

3,470 acres, KDWP, (620) 241-7669
Ongoing effort to restore significant portions of some fifty large and small prairie marshlands that rivaled Cheyenne Bottoms before many were drained at the turn of the century.

Obtain map and information at headquarters: from McPherson, go west 7 miles on Highway 56 to Conway, then follow signs north to Mohawk, then go east 1.5 miles.

16 Maxwell Wildlife Refuge and McPherson State Fishing Lake

2,560 acres, KDWP, (620) 628-4455
Tallgrass prairie at the western edge of its limit. Fine wildflower displays in summer. Observation tower for viewing bison and elk.

From Canton, go north 6 miles on County Road 304.

17 The Land Institute

(785) 823-5376
The Land Institute takes its cue from the prairie. For this reason, its mission provides an important complement to the native prairies in this guide. Its major program, called Natural Systems Agriculture, uses the prairie as a model of ecological stability to devise a new form of agriculture that sustains natural resources and rural communities.

On I-135 just south of Salina, take Exit 89 (Schilling Road), go east 1 mile to stoplight, south 1 mile on 9th Street (Old Highway 81), then east 2.5 miles on East Water Well Road. Self-guided tours, Monday–Friday, 8 a.m.–5 p.m. Guided tours, Tuesday and Friday, 3 p.m. (reservations required). Prairie festival held annually.

THE FLINT HILLS

Approximately 5 million acres

The Flint Hills, stretching from north of Manhattan to the Kansas-Oklahoma border, form a monolithic spinal column of rocky, grass-covered knolls. They encompass our last great stand of tallgrass prairie. Flinty soils impeded the plow, so the hills became the domain of ranching. The region is crisscrossed with numerous scenic byways, including Highway 177 from Manhattan to Cottonwood Falls. The following seven sites provide public access.

18 Tuttle Creek Reservoir and Wildlife Area

26,800 acres, USACE, (785) 539-8511; KDWP, (785) 539-7941
Upland tallgrass prairie. Good birding area.

From Manhattan, go north 4.5 miles on Highway 177. USACE information center is west of dam. State park office is below dam on east side.

19 Konza Prairie Biological Station

8,616 acres, Kansas State University, (785) 539-1961, (785) 532-6620; TNC, (785) 233-4400
Established as a research site in 1972. Konza Prairie is one of twenty-four research sites in North America participating in the National Science Foundation's Long Term Ecological Research Network, which studies ecological phenomena and processes over broad spatial and temporal scales. Six miles of public trails wend through a portion of the tallgrass prairie and gallery forests and afford stunning vistas of the Flint Hills. Much of site is closed to public because of ongoing research.

From Manhattan, take Highway 177 south, cross the Kansas River, turn west on McDowell Creek Road (County Road 901) and go 6.4 miles, then go south .25 mile to gravel parking area.

20 Tallgrass Prairie National Preserve

10,894 acres, NPS, National Park Trust, (620) 273-8494
A lovely exploration of the natural and cultural history of the Flint Hills and a poignant tribute to the tallgrass biome. Visitors can walk onto the tallgrass prairie on the Southwind Nature Trail, take a bus tour of the surrounding area, and stroll through the historic Springhill Ranch headquarters, which includes an 1880s Victorian ranch house and a massive stone barn.

From Strong City, take Highway 177 north 2 miles.

21 Flint Hills Tallgrass Prairie Preserve

2,188 acres, TNC, (785) 233-4400
Prairie contains portion of headwaters of South Fork of Cottonwood River.

Located approximately 6 miles east of Cassoday. Contact TNC for field trip information.

22 Flint Hills National Wildlife Refuge

18,463 acres, USDA-FS, (316) 392-5553
Diverse landscape that includes tallgrass prairie and wetland complexes. Name is a misnomer since refuge actually lies east of the Flint Hills in the limestone-and-shale Osage Cuestas.

From Emporia, go east on I-35 to Exit 141, then south 8 miles on Highway 130 to refuge headquarters in Hartford.

23 Welda Prairie Preserve

128 acres, TNC, (785) 233-4400
Biologically diverse prairie that is also a study site for one of the world's largest populations of threatened Mead's milkweed.

Located between Welda and Garnett. Contact TNC for field trip information.

24 Haskell-Baker Wetlands

573 acres, Baker University, (785) 594-6451
Remnant marsh and wet prairie in floodplain of Wakarusa River on edge of Lawrence. Fine example of a natural area in an urban context. A National Natural Landmark.

In Lawrence, from intersection of Highway 59 and Highway 10, go south 1.5 miles to 31st Street, turn east and go 1.5 miles.

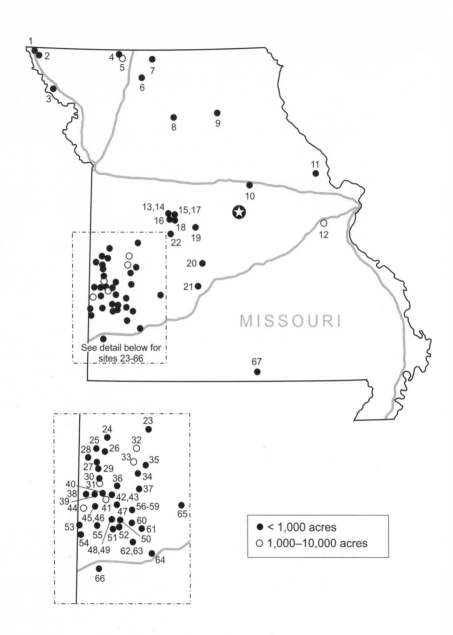

See detail below for sites 23-66

MISSOURI

● < 1,000 acres
○ 1,000–10,000 acres

MISSOURI

The great American artist and Missouri native son Thomas Hart Benton is the source of my favorite remark about prairie space. "For me," he wrote, "the Great Plains have a releasing effect. They make me want to run and shout at the top of my voice. I like their endlessness. I like the way they make human beings appear as the little bugs they really are." In Missouri, it is still possible to run and shout at the top of one's voice on a number of see-forever prairies, especially on the Osage Plains, which now harbor the majority of the state's 70,000 acres of remaining prairie.

Missouri prairies once flourished across three distinct landforms: the Loess Hills, which taper into northwestern Missouri from Iowa like the tip of a tyrannosaurus tail; the Glaciated Plains, which are simply an extension of the Southern Iowa Drift Plain; and the Osage Plains, a cherty, thin-soiled landscape that escaped the powerful force of glaciation. Jon Hawker, in *Missouri Landscapes: A Tour through Time*, describes how all these landforms came to be, and his explanations of the evolution of the grassland biome and of the four great glacial stages during the Ice Age are as clear and concise as any I have read on these important topics.

THE LOESS HILLS

This peculiar skeletal landform, which defines the entire western border of Iowa, extends some 40 miles into northwestern Missouri. It is exhilarating to scramble around on Loess Hills prairies—I've gotten a little dizzy on a few ridge tops—and in addition they provide lofty views of surrounding terrain. See the Iowa chapter for a thumbnail description of the Loess Hills.

1 Star School Hill Prairie Natural Area

70 acres, MDC, (816) 271-3100

For travelers on I-29 who would like to stretch a leg, this rugged little swath of Loess Hills prairie is easily accessible and highly recommended.

On I-29 in Iowa, take Exit 1 to Hamburg, then Highway 275 south. Prairie is 1.5 miles south of the Iowa-Missouri state line where Highway 275 runs parallel to I-29.

2 Brickyard Hill Loess Mound Natural Area

125 acres, MDC, (816) 271-3100

Dramatic canted prairie landscape with 200-foot gradient.

On I-29 in Missouri, take Exit 116. Prairie is just east of junction of I-29 and Highway A; Highway RA forms western boundary of conservation area.

3 McCormack Loess Mound Natural Area

158 acres, TNC, (314) 968-1105; MDC, (816) 271-3100

Another opportunity to scale a near-vertical Loess Hills prairie. A visit in October combines golden autumnal grasses and abundant migratory waterfowl at adjacent 7,178-acre Squaw Creek National Wildlife Refuge.

From I-29, take Exit 79 west on Highway 159 for 3 miles to parking area on east side of road.

THE GLACIATED PLAINS

The Glaciated Plains are an extension of the Southern Iowa Drift Plain, an old, weathered landscape of undulating hills formed by erosion since the last glacial activity 200,000 years ago. The Glaciated Plains cover the northern tier of Missouri and are bounded on the south by the Missouri River; on a map, the plains resemble icing draping over the side of a cake. This was the heart of the tallgrass prairie in Missouri and, like tallgrass just about everywhere, most of it is gone. What remains is a canvas for creative restoration.

4 Pawnee Prairie Preserve/Pawnee Prairie Conservation Area

909 acres, TNC, (660) 867-3866; MDC, (816) 271-3100

Large expanse of tallgrass prairie. Supports classic array of grassland songbirds—bobolink, sedge wren, upland sandpiper, greater prairie-chicken—with peak activity in June. Comprises two adjoining tracts (434 acres owned by TNC, 475 by MDC) that are being actively restored. With nearby Dunn Ranch (see below), it is the nucleus of the Pawnee Prairie Focus Area, approximately 25,000 acres in which MDC and TNC are working with willing private landowners to enhance grassland habitat.

From Hatfield, take gravel road in town south .5 mile.

5 Dunn Ranch

4,000 acres, TNC, (660) 867-3866

Ambitious tallgrass prairie conservation and restoration project in conjunction with similar effort on nearby Pawnee Prairie (see above). Focal point of Dunn Ranch is thousand-acre core area that has never been plowed and represents the largest native tallgrass prairie site within the Glaciated Plains. Some or all parts of preserve may be temporarily closed for restoration work, so please contact TNC prior to visiting.

In Eagleville, from intersection of Highway 69 and Highway M, go west 5 miles on Highway M, then north on 180th Avenue. Dunn Ranch lies on both sides of the road.

6 Helton Prairie Natural Area

30 acres, MDC, (816) 271-3100

Small, off-the-beaten-path prairie but worth the trip because it harbors an especially high diversity of wildflowers.

From Bethany, take Highway 136 east 9 miles to Highway CC. Follow it east and then south 3 miles, then turn west on gravel road and go 1.75 miles. Prairie is in extreme northwest corner of Wayne Helton Memorial Wildlife Area.

7 Chloe Lowry Marsh Natural Area

115 acres, MDC, (816) 271-3100

Highly diverse marsh and wet prairie.

From Highway 136, on west edge of Princeton, take Highway FF north 2 miles, then go west and north 2 miles on gravel road leading to Lowry Memorial Airport.

8 Cordgrass Bottoms Natural Area and Locust Creek Prairie

880 acres in two tracts, MDNR, *Pershing State Park, (660) 963-2299*

Two nearby sites situated on Locust Creek, a tributary of the Grand River, form a lovely juxtaposition of wet prairie, marsh, and floodplain forest. The 800-acre Locust Creek Prairie is the largest extant riparian wet prairie on the Glaciated Plains; it has an excellent interpretive trail and boardwalk. Located at the north end of Pershing State Park.

From Chillicothe, go 20 miles east on Highway 36 to Highway 130 and follow signs to park.

9 Bee Trace and Little Chariton Grasslands

300 acres in several tracts, MDNR, *(660) 773-5229*

One of the handful of tallgrass prairies remaining on the Glaciated Plains. Both areas are in Long Branch State Park. Bee Trace encompasses several scattered native prairie tracts totaling 200 acres; largest remnant is 30 acres. It is located on a peninsula in north part of park. The 100-acre Little Chariton Grasslands borders campground and is easily accessible.

Bee Trace: In Macon, at intersection of Highway 36 and Highway 63, go north 5 miles on Highway 63, then west 2 miles on gravel road to park sign. Little Chariton: From Macon, take Highway 36 west 2 miles to park, proceed to campground.

10 Tucker Prairie

146 acres, University of Missouri, (573) 882-4717

A glimpse of tallgrass prairie on I-70 about 19 miles east of Columbia. Don't blink. Prairie is a research station for University of Missouri and is open to public. A National Natural Landmark.

South side of I-70, 2.5 miles west of intersection of I-70 and Highway 54.

11 Sherwood, Sac, Northwoods, and Dry Branch Prairies

123 acres in four tracts, MDNR, *Cuivre River State Park, (636) 528-7247*

Small prairie pockets—largest is 70-acre Sherwood Prairie—scattered in Lincoln Hills, an isolated arc of hills rising from the Glaciated Plains. Located within Cuivre River State Park.

From Troy, take Highway 47 east 3 miles, then go north on Highway 147 to park entrance. Inquire at visitors' center for locations of prairies.

12 Shaw Nature Reserve

2,500 acres, Missouri Botanical Garden, (636) 451-3512

Shaw Nature Reserve is an arboretum of managed plantings, including many native Missouri species. It also focuses on research and application of habitat restoration techniques, including the study of fire ecology. About half of the reserve's acreage is devoted to restoration of tallgrass prairie, glade, and wetland habitats, which serve as educational landscapes for conservation of our diminished grassland biome.

From St. Louis, take I-44 southwest about 30 miles to Exit 353 in Gray Summit. Follow signs to nature reserve.

THE OSAGE PLAINS

The Osage Plains, in west central Missouri, are a physiographic area where prairie watchers could spend many happy days exploring back roads and byways in quest of an array of beautiful remnant grasslands. Unlike landscapes to the north, this area was never glaciated. The soils, rather than being thick, rich glacial deposits ideal for farming, are the result of erosion of rock. In many places in the Osage Plains, the bedrock lies near the soil surface, making the land difficult to cultivate. Hence, many prairies remained unplowed. The Osage Plains extend into Kansas (where their finest expression is the Flint Hills), through central Oklahoma, and then taper off in north central Texas.

The Osage Plains border the forested Ozark Uplift to the east and consequently are an area where prairie and woodland intermingle and shift dominance over time. The last entry in the Missouri section—

Tingler Lake Wet-Mesic Prairie—is situated in the Ozark Uplift and demonstrates this ecological transition.

The following seven prairies are neighbors, making visits to all convenient. They are for the most part dry-mesic upland tallgrass prairies characterized by cherty limestone and shale soils. Wildflowers are impressive in spring and summer. Additional notes are included under some of the entries.

13 Grandfather Prairie Conservation Area

78 acres, MDC, (660) 885-6981

Name commemorates the Osage, whose tribal members called the sun Grandfather.

From Sedalia, go south about 8 miles on Highway 65, then west 2 miles on Mather Road.

14 Friendly Prairie

40 acres, MPF, (888) 843-6739

The name comes from the fact that this site used to serve as a rest stop for highway travelers.

From Sedalia, go south about 9 miles on Highway 65, then west 1.25 miles on Manila Road.

15 Paint Brush Prairie Conservation Area

314 acres, MDC, (660) 885-6981

A 74-acre tract in northwest corner of conservation area has been designated as Paint Brush Prairie Natural Area.

From Sedalia, go south about 10 miles on Highway 65, then east on Manila Road. The prairie lies on either side of the road.

16 Drovers' Prairie

80 acres in two tracts, MPF, (888) 843-6739

The southwestern tract is flat mesic-wet prairie along Henry Creek.

From Sedalia, go south about 10 miles on Highway 65, then west 1 mile on Highway 52. Prairie is on south side of road in two 40-acre tracts.

17 Goodnight-Henry Prairie

40 acres, TNC, (314) 968-1105
From Sedalia, go south about 7 miles on Highway 65, east 3 miles on Highway V, then south .25 mile on Highway U.

18 Hi Lonesome Prairie Conservation Area

627 acres, MDC, (660) 885-6981
One of the largest tallgrass remnants on the Osage Plains.
From Cole Camp, go west 1 mile on Highway 52, then north .5 mile on County Road NE 221.

19 Hite Prairie Conservation Area

102 acres, MDC, (660) 885-6981
Upland prairie where Ozarks blend into Osage Plains.
On southwest edge of Versailles, .5 mile south of Highway 52. Prairie is situated west of fairgrounds.

20 Ha Ha Tonka Savanna Natural Area

953 acres, MDNR, Ha Ha Tonka State Park, (573) 346-2986
Chert, dolomite, sandstone savanna, and dolomite glades, where native Osage Plains prairie intermingles with Ozarks woodlands. A 7-mile trail goes through natural area. Largest publicly accessible savanna in Missouri, located within Ha Ha Tonka State Park.
From Camdenton, go southwest 2.5 miles on Highway 54 to park entrance.

21 Bennett Spring Savanna

920 acres, TNC, (314) 968-1105
Savanna of oak and hickory intermingled with tallgrass prairie. Sprawls across rugged ravines within the recharge zone of Bennett Springs. One of the largest remaining intact Ozarks savannas. Because of steep terrain ravines and lack of designated trails, visitors should carry map and compass or ask TNC about guided fieldtrips.
From Lebanon, go west about 9 miles on Highway 64 to Bennett Spring State Park. Continue west through the park on Highway 64A,

then go south 6 miles on Highway OO. Look for preserve sign and gravel turnout.

22 Rock Hill Prairie

68 acres, TNC, (314) 968-1105
Active restoration of glade and prairie mosaic.
From Warsaw, go about 6 miles north on Highway 65 to Highway BB. Prairie is east of Highway 65 and south of Highway BB.

23 Chapel View Prairie Conservation Area

384 acres, MDC, (660) 885-6981
Upland prairie managed primarily as greater prairie-chicken habitat.
From Deepwater, go west 2.5 miles on Highway 52, south 2 miles on Highway F, then west .5 mile on County Road SW 1000.

THE OSAGE CLUSTER

The following forty-three sites form another impressive cluster of grasslands on the Osage Plains—Ozarks cusp and comprise one of the best prairie-hopping circuits in this guide. Be prepared to travel gravel roads and do some backtracking when you miss a turn.

24 Ripgut Prairie Conservation Area

280 acres, MDC, (660) 885-6981
Named for razor-sharp prairie cordgrass, a major constituent of wet prairies, which cuts bellies of horses and legs of improperly clad prairie watchers. Site is being actively restored.
From Highway 71 on east edge of Rich Hill, go east on Highway B .75 mile, then follow gravel road north and east about 1.5 miles (roads are marked with signs to prairie).

25 Gama Grass Prairie Conservation Area

80 acres, MDC, (660) 885-6981
Hardpan prairie supports Missouri's largest extant stand of native eastern gama grass.

From Rich Hill, go south 4 miles on Highway 71, then west 1 mile on gravel road.

26 Horton Bottoms Natural Area

227 acres, MDC, (660) 885-6981

Bottomland complex of wet prairie, wet savanna, marsh, and forest on Little Osage River. Located in southwestern corner of Four Rivers Conservation Area. Access is best by boat.

Entrance to conservation area: From Rich Hill, go south about 3 miles on Highway 71, east 1 mile on Highway TT, then south 2.5 miles on gravel road. Contact MDC regarding access to natural area.

27 Douglas Branch Conservation Area

360 acres, MDC, (660) 885-6981

One of the few Missouri prairies accessible to the public that shows the vital connection between bottomland and upland prairies, a linkage that has largely been severed on North American grasslands.

From Nevada, go north about 6 miles on Highway 71, then west .33 mile on gravel road, following signs to parking lot.

28 Stilwell Prairie

376 acres, MPF, (888) 843-6739

Curvaceous landforms, high plant diversity. Degraded areas being actively restored.

From Richards, go east 1 mile on Highway H, then north 1 mile on gravel road.

29 Marmaton River Bottoms Wet Prairie

609 acres, TNC, (314) 968-1105

Largest known unplowed wet prairie in Missouri. Encompasses cordgrass prairie and bottomlands of pecan, hickory, bur oak, and pin oak. Old fields being actively restored.

In Nevada, from intersection of Highway 71 and Highway W, go north on Highway W (Ash Street). About .5 mile after passing state hospital (on west side of Highway W), continue north 1 mile on small road (do not take Highway W, which turns west at this point). At T intersection, go west and follow this winding road north and then west (you will cross the Marmaton River) to the first road heading south. Take this road about .5 mile to north boundary of preserve.

30 Little Osage Prairie Natural Area

80 acres, TNC, (314) 968-1105

Small unit with great plant diversity across road from larger Osage Prairie.

From Nevada, go south 6 miles on Highway 71, then west 1.5 miles on gravel road.

31 Osage Prairie Conservation Area

1,506 acres, MDC, (660) 885-6981

Big chunk of upland prairie encompassing three stream sheds. Much of land originally acquired by TNC via Katherine Ordway funds.

From Nevada, take Highway 71 south 6 miles, west .5 mile on gravel road, then south .5 mile on another gravel road.

32 Taberville Prairie Conservation Area

1,680 acres, MDC, (660) 885-6981

Another prairie gem on the Osage Plains. Large and lovely expanse of upland prairie with sandstone outcrops and a spring-fed stream. Home to one of Missouri's largest populations of greater prairie-chickens. A National Natural Landmark.

From Appleton City, go east .5 mile on Highway 52, south 2 miles on Highway A, then south 7 miles on Highway H.

33 Wah'Kon-Tah Prairie

4,771 acres, MDC and TNC, (417) 876-2340

Magnificent stand of tallgrass prairie on gently rolling hills, the largest and farthest east in North America. Named for one of the Osage tribes. Some or all parts of preserve may be temporarily closed for restoration work, so please contact TNC prior to visit.

From El Dorado Springs, go north and east about 3 miles on Highway 82. Where Highway 82 intersects Highway H, take gravel road to the right and go up incline to preserve sign.

34 Monegaw Prairie Conservation Area

270 acres, TNC, (314) 968-1105; MDC, (660) 885-6981
Upland prairie with permanent spring. Named for Osage chief.
From El Dorado Springs, go east about 2.5 miles on Highway 54. Prairie is on south side of highway.

35 Schwartz Prairie

240 acres, MPF, (888) 843-6739
Upland prairie and sandstone glade named for conservationists Charles and Elizabeth Schwartz.
From El Dorado Springs, go north and east about 8 miles on Highway 82 to Tiffin. Continue east 5 miles on Highway 82 and south 2 miles on Highway K. Where Highway K jogs east, continue south 1 mile on gravel road, then west .25 mile on gravel road.

36 Gay Feather Prairie

116 acres, MDC and MPF, (888) 843-6739
Upland prairie named for gay feather (genus *Liatris*), a bold purple wildflower that blooms in late summer.
From Milo, go east about 7.5 miles on Highway E, then south 2 miles on gravel road.

37 Sky Prairie Conservation Area

200 acres, MDC, (417) 895-6880
Sky Prairie is named for the ridge top views a visitor may attain on this upland prairie. Long ridge with deep wooded ravines runs diagonally across the prairie.
From El Dorado Springs, go south and east about 12.5 miles on Highway 32 through Filley. Where Highway 32 intersects Highway CC and goes east, continue south 2.75 miles on gravel road, then west 1 mile on gravel road.

38 Comstock Prairie Conservation Area

320 acres, MDC, (417) 895-6880
Prairie-shrub landscape named for wooded stream running through it.

From Bronaugh, go south about 2.75 miles on Highway 43, then west 1 mile on NW 100 Road.

39 Bushwhacker Prairie

665 acres in two tracts, MDC, (660) 885-6981

Upland prairie, draw, and wooded stream within Bushwhacker Lake Conservation Area.

From Bronaugh, go south about 2.75 miles on Highway 43, then east 1 mile on NW 100 Road.

40 Lattner Prairie and Edgar and Ruth Denison Prairie

240 acres in two tracts, MPF, (888) 843-6739

Two adjacent upland grasslands named for prairie patrons.

From Sheldon, go about 3 miles west on Highway N, south 1.5 miles on gravel road, then east .25 mile on NW 100 Road. Lattner Prairie is on north side of road, Denison Prairie on south side.

41 Buffalo Wallow Prairie Conservation Area

1,113 acres in two tracts, MDC, (417) 895-6880

Upland prairie and old croplands in process of returning to native vegetation.

From Sheldon, go south 3 miles on Highway 71 to main tract; go west 1 mile on NW 80th Road to smaller tract.

42 Clear Creek Conservation Area

762 acres, MDC, (417) 895-6880

About 380 acres of upland prairie associated with oak-hickory woodlands.

From just west of Sheldon, go south 3 miles on Highway 71, east 4 miles on NE 80th Road, then north 1 mile on NE 40th Lane.

43 Edward B. and Marie O. Risch Conservation Area

163 acres, MDC, (417) 895-6880

Hilly upland prairie with 40-acre wildlife food plot. Named after donors.

From just west of Sheldon, go south 3 miles on Highway 71, east 4 miles on NE 80th Road, north 1 mile on NE 40th Lane, then east 1 mile on NE 90th Road.

44 Prairie State Park

3,702 acres, MDNR, (417) 843-6711

Beautiful landscape of rolling upland tallgrass prairie, headwater streams, wetlands, sandstone outcrops, and roaming bison and elk. Numerous field trips and interpretive programs make this park an ideal introduction to the tallgrass prairie.

From Lamar, go west 16 miles on Highway 160, north 1 mile on Highway NN, west 3 miles on W. Central Road, then north 1.3 miles to visitors' center.

45 Redwing Prairie Conservation Area

160 acres, MDC, (417) 895-6880

Upland prairie.

From Liberal, go east 4 miles on NW 30th Road.

46 Mo-No-I Prairie Conservation Area

302 acres, MDC, (417) 895-6880

Upland prairie adjacent to privately owned grassland of similar size forms almost a full section, making this one of the most impressive prairie remnants in Missouri. Name is Osage word for greater prairie-chicken.

From Lamar, go west about 4 miles to Highway W, then north through Iantha about 3.5 miles on Highway W, then east .5 mile on Highway DD.

47 Pawhuska Prairie Natural Area

77 acres, TNC, (314) 968-1105

Upland prairie with permanent spring. Name is Osage for white-haired.

From Lamar, go east 6.5 miles on Highway 160, north 3 miles on Highway HH, then west .5 mile on NE 30th Road.

48 Treaty Line Prairie Conservation Area

168 acres, MDC, (417) 895-6880

Upland prairie bisected by draw. In Treaty of 1808, Osage ceded lands east of line from Fort Osage to Fort Smith, Arkansas.

From Lamar, take Highway 160 east 2 miles, go south 1.5 miles on SE 40th Lane, then east .5 mile on SE 20th Road.

49 Pa Sole Prairie Conservation Area

240 acres, MDC, (417) 895-6880

Contains remnant 94-acre upland prairie featuring high mound of cap rock sandstone. Name is Osage phrase for settlers on hilltops.

From just west of Lamar, go south 6 miles on Highway 71, east 5 miles on Highway 126, then north 1.25 miles on SE 50th Lane.

50 Shelton L. Cook Memorial Meadow

301 acres, TNC, (314) 968-1105

Array of prairie types, resulting from underlying variety of soils. Noted for its high floral diversity.

From Golden City, go north about 2 miles on Highway 160, then west 2 miles on Highway U.

51 Dorris Creek Prairie Conservation Area

160 acres, MDC, (417) 895-6880

Upland prairie with three small lakes.

From Golden City, go west 7 miles on Highway 126, then south 1 mile on SE 40th Lane.

52 Golden Prairie

320 acres, MPF, (888) 843-6739

Rolling upland prairie cut by two draws. A National Natural Landmark.

From Golden City, go south 2 miles on Highway 37, then west 3 miles on SE 90th Road.

53 Mon-Shon Prairie Conservation Area

80 acres, MDC, (417) 895-6880

Upland prairie with rich flora. Name is Osage for sacred earth.

From Highway 126 on Missouri-Kansas border, go south 2.5 miles on SW State Line Lane.

54 Wah-Sha-She Prairie Natural Area

160 acres, TNC, (314) 968-1105

Flat hardpan prairie and wildlife refuge with marsh and constructed pond. Name means Water People, a group of the Osage.

From Asbury, go north 2 miles on Highway 171, east .8 mile on Highway M, then north .2 mile on 30th Road to parking lot.

55 Bethel Prairie

260 acres, MDC, (417) 895-6880

Upland prairie cut by seasonal branch of North Fork of Spring River.

From Jasper, go north 4 miles on Highway 71, then west 4 miles on Highway 126. Prairie is on south side of road.

56 Stony Point Prairie Conservation Area

640 acres, MDC, (417) 895-6880

Upland prairie with sandstone outcrops.

From Lockwood, go north 8 miles on Highway 97, west 4 miles on Highway E, then north 1 mile on Highway D.

57 Burns Tract

320 acres, MPF, (888) 843-6739

Rolling upland prairie adjoining Stony Point Prairie on east.

From Lockwood, go north 8 miles on Highway 97, west 4 miles on Highway E, then north 1 mile on Highway D.

58 Niawathe Prairie Conservation Area

320 acres, TNC and MDC, (417) 895-6880

Upland prairie known for showy spring wildflowers. Ni-Wa-The was the Life-Giver of the Sky People of the Osage.

From Lockwood, go north 8 miles on Highway 97, west 1 mile on Highway E, then north .5 mile on gravel road.

59 Penn-Sylvania Prairie

160 acres, MPF, (888) 843-6739

Upland prairie with two ponds attractive to migratory waterfowl.

From Lockwood, go north 8 miles on Highway 97, west 2 miles on Highway E, then south about 1 mile on gravel road. Prairie is on west side of road.

60 Horse Creek Prairie Conservation Area

80 acres, MDC, (417) 895-6880

Flat upland prairie with abundant spring wildflowers.

From Lockwood, go west 2 miles on Highway 160, then north 1 mile on gravel road.

61 Indigo Prairie Conservation Area

40 acres, MDC, (417) 895-6880

Upland prairie and shrub communities named for blue-flowered *Baptisia* growing on site.

From Lockwood, take Highway 97 south 1 mile, go east 2.5 miles on unmarked gravel road.

62 Providence Prairie Conservation Area

197 acres, MDC, (417) 895-6880

Mesic prairie with permanent spring and small stream. According to *Public Prairies of Missouri*, "It appeared that this prairie was destined for the plow, but by providence this did not occur."

From intersection of Highway 96 and Highway 97, go north 6.5 miles on Highway 97, west 1.5 miles on Highway NN, then south 1 mile on County Road 1040.

63 Kickapoo Prairie Conservation Area

160 acres, MDC, (417) 895-6880

Upland prairie with numerous draws. The Kickapoo once occupied land west of Springfield.

From intersection of Highway 96 and Highway 97, go north 2 miles on Highway 97, then west 1 mile on County Road 2040.

64 Mount Vernon Prairie Natural Area

40 acres, TNC, (314) 968-1105

Upland dry prairie with showy wildflowers.

From Mt. Vernon, go north 1 mile on Highway 39, east 1.2 miles on Highway 174, north 1 mile on County Road 1140, east about .9 mile on County Road 2100, then north about .3 mile to preserve parking lot on west side of road.

65 La Petite Gemme Natural Area

37 acres, MPF, (888) 843-6739

Small but exquisite (hence the name) landscape of limestone-dolomite prairie on knob slopes, acidic hardpan prairie, and seeps supporting fen plants. The 30-mile rail-to-trail Ozark Highland Trail crosses the area.

From Bolivar, go south 3 miles on Highway 83 (also called Business Highway 13) to intersection with Highway 13. Continue south on Highway 13 about .75 mile to first gravel road going west; take this road 1 mile west. Prairie lies south of road.

66 Diamond Grove Prairie Natural Area

611 acres, MDC, (417) 895-6880

Flat to gently rolling upland prairie with lovely, diverse flora.

From Diamond, go west 4 miles on Highway V, then north 1.25 miles on Lark Road. Prairie lies east of road.

67 Tingler Lake Wet-Mesic Prairie

10 acres, MDC, (417) 256-7161

Small and extremely rare prairie remnant in the Missouri Ozarks with high plant diversity and sinkhole pond; trails make area user-friendly. Lies within 240-acre Tingler Lake Conservation Area, of which 145 acres are being restored to prairie.

From West Plains, go about 6 miles south on Highway 17, west on County Road 910 to County Road 811, then south about .3 mile on County Road 811 to conservation area access.

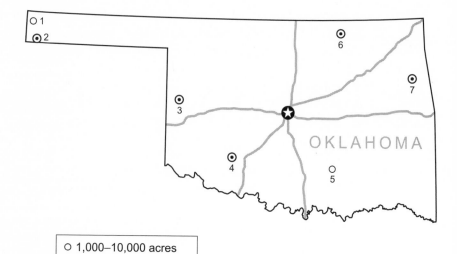

○ 1,000–10,000 acres
⊙ 10,000–100,000 acres

OKLAHOMA

September 16, 1893, can be considered the commencement of the full-scale consumption of Oklahoma's natural resources. On that day an estimated 100,000 white settlers waited at several locations along the Kansas state line for the cavalry gunshots and bugle calls that would signal the start of the Cherokee Outlet Land Rush. The federal government had purchased a 6-million-acre swath of land in Oklahoma Territory from the Cherokees and subdivided it into 40,000 homesteads. It is said that by dawn of the next day all the land had been claimed. In little more than a century, 70 percent of Oklahoma's prairies have been lost or seriously disturbed. Oklahomans, however, can take pride in a particularly dazzling grassland conservation achievement, the Nature Conservancy's 39,000-acre Tallgrass Prairie Preserve, north of Pawhuska. It is the largest protected area of tallgrass in North America.

The beauty of Oklahoma lies in its folded and faulted topography. There are three principal mountain ranges in the southern part of the state—the Wichita, Arbuckle, and Ouachita—and numerous lesser ones scattered about—such as the Hi Early and Rattlesnake Mountains. In addition, there are the Glass Mountain badlands in the northwest and the deeply incised Ozark Plateau in the northeast. In contrast to the soothing, undulating grasslands of the glacial landscapes to the north, Oklahoma's prairies are more often associated with rugged ground, and perhaps the most beautiful convergence of grass and rough-and-tumble terrain is found at Wichita Mountains National Wildlife Refuge.

1 Black Mesa Preserve

1,600 acres, Oklahoma Tourism and Recreation Department,
(580) 261-7447 (contact number is for Kenton Mercantile, small store
near preserve)
Short-grass prairie atop dramatic mesa, which is an easternmost geologic finger of Rocky Mountains.

From Boise City, go west 35 miles on Highway 325, then north 5 miles on blacktop road (sign marked "Colorado"). Parking area on west side of road.

2 Rita Blanca National Grassland

93,323 acres, USDA-FS, (505) 374-9652

Mixed-grass prairie reclaimed from 1930s Dust Bowl. Straddles Oklahoma and Texas and is adjacent to Kiowa National Grassland in New Mexico.

From Dalhart, Texas, go north 25 miles on Highway 385.

3 Black Kettle National Grassland

31,300 acres, USDA-FS, (580) 497-2143

Part of federal 1930s Dust Bowl reclamation. Rolling hills of short-grass and mixed-grass prairie, with oak thickets. Named for Black Kettle, a Southern Cheyenne chief who was killed on November 27, 1868, along with his wife and numerous kin, in an engagement with Lt. Col. George Custer known as Battle of Washita. Grassland usage includes recreational opportunities as well as cattle grazing and oil drilling. An additional 1,449 acres of this grassland are in Texas.

From I-40, take Sayre exit (20), go north 25 miles on Highway 283 to Cheyenne, then west on Highway 47. Cross bridge and go .5 mile to district office at intersection of Highway 47 and Highway 47A. Battle of Washita National Historic Site is nearby on Highway 47A.

4 Wichita Mountains National Wildlife Refuge

59,020 acres, USFWS, (580) 429-3222

Exquisite grasslands (exhibiting attributes of tall-, mixed-, and short-grass prairie) intermingle with oak thickets against dramatic background of craggy red granite mountains. Rugged terrain provided concealment and a last redoubt for Plains Indians in late 1800s, which explains proximity of Fort Sill. An early example of federal involvement in land protection, the preserve was established in 1901 and bison were reintroduced in 1907. Elk, longhorns, prairie dogs, and both eastern and western birds abound.

From Lawton, go west 25 miles on Highway 62, then north on Highway 115 to refuge.

5 Pontotoc Ridge

2,900 acres, TNC, (580) 777-2224

Tallgrass and mixed-grass prairie, streams, springs, hardwood forest, and post oak–blackjack oak woodlands. The latter form part of the Cross Timbers, which once stretched from southeastern Kansas through central Oklahoma to northeastern Texas. Preserve is situated on eastern flank of geological formation called the Arbuckle Uplift. Three-mile prairie trail provides wildflower viewing and vistas.

From intersection of Highway 99/377 and Highway 99A, just south of Fittstown, go south 7.3 miles on Highway 99/377 to Pontotoc Road (on Pontotoc-Johnson county line). Go east on this road, which in about 1 mile turns north. Continue north and look for the double gate at the preserve entrance.

6 Tallgrass Prairie Preserve

39,000 acres, TNC, (918) 287-4803

Great vistas of grass and sky. Preserve is largest protected tallgrass prairie in North America. Ambitious efforts under way to restore original ecosystem driven by fire and bison. Free-ranging bison can often be seen on the 35-mile driving route through preserve, which is open daily from dawn to dusk. Visitor center, hiking trails, and picnicking at historic ranch headquarters. Contact TNC about guided hikes on weekends.

From intersection of Highway 60 and Kihekah Avenue in Pawhuska, follow signs to preserve.

7 J. T. Nickel Family Nature and Wildlife Preserve

15,000 acres, TNC, (918) 585-1117, (918) 456-7601

A large landscape donated to TNC in late 1990s by the J. T. Nickel family. Formerly the J-5 Ranch. Preserve, which adjoins Illinois River, is predominantly Ozark pine and oak forests but includes impressive oak savanna and tallgrass prairie. Public may drive the main east-west road through the preserve; hiking trails are available by reservation. Call above numbers for general information; call (918) 585-1117 to make trail reservations.

From intersection of Highway 82 and Highway 62/51, on east edge of Tahlequah, go east 5.2 miles on Highway 62/51, north 3.1 miles on Oakdale Drive, then continue north 6 miles on gravel road. Preserve entrance is at large timber gate.

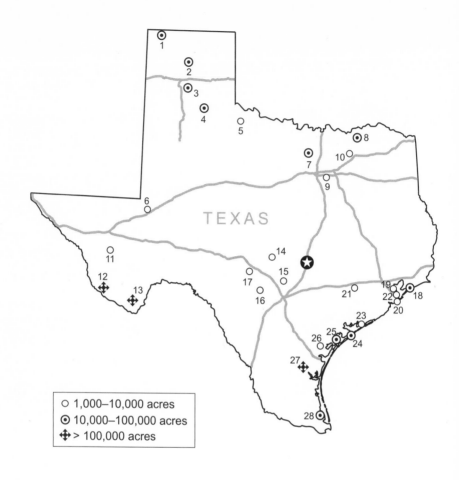

○ 1,000–10,000 acres
◉ 10,000–100,000 acres
✛ > 100,000 acres

TEXAS

I was born in Mitchell County, Texas, on the Rolling Plains, a natural region that lies at the southern end of the Great Plains. I like to think now that when I was a child standing in my front yard in Colorado City I was looking all the way to Canada. I also assume the happenstance of birth accounts for a preference for the subtle, horizontal landscapes where prairies once flourished. However, by the time I was born, in 1946, Texas grasslands had already taken a beating by way of nineteenth-century overstocking of livestock, sod busting for farming, and the suppression of natural fires. Three decades later, by the time I was cognizant of prairies, the situation would be compounded by suburban sprawl, invasion of alien plant species, the ranchette phenomenon, and groundwater and aquifer depletion.

Texas is typically divided into eleven natural regions, ten of which include grasslands of one sort or another. A lovely color map of these regions can be found via this portal: www.tpwd.state.tx.us/nature. Seven of the regions are cited below, because they provide a logical framework for visiting prairies.

HIGH PLAINS/ROLLING PLAINS

Together these two physiographic regions comprise what is otherwise known as the Texas Panhandle. Lying to the west are the High Plains, a vast tabletop of short-grass prairie that supported huge ranches in the nineteenth century but is now largely dedicated to irrigated fields of cotton, wheat, and sorghum. The eastern edge of the High Plains, called the Caprock Escarpment, is a dramatic eroded precipice that more or less bisects the Panhandle from north to south. On its eastern flank are the Rolling Plains, which are just that—oceanic swells of mixed-grass and tallgrass prairie dissected by rugged, scenic canyonlands.

1 Rita Blanca National Grassland

93,323 acres, USDA-FS, (505) 374-9652

Mixed-grass prairie reclaimed from 1930s Dust Bowl. Straddles Oklahoma and Texas and is adjacent to Kiowa National Grassland in New Mexico. Purists note that the better examples of grassland are in New Mexico. One observer remarks: "Go to the Texas line and look west."

From Dalhart, go north 25 miles on Highway 385.

2 Lake Meredith National Recreation Area

45,000 acres, NPS, (806) 857-3151

Mixed-grass prairie in scenic Canadian River breaks. Water sports and fishing are the primary recreational activities at the 21,600-acre reservoir.

From Amarillo, go north 38 miles on Highway 136. Park headquarters: 419 E. Broadway in Fritch.

3 Palo Duro Canyon State Park

16,402 acres, TPWD, (806) 488-2227

Dramatic badlands landscapes along upper tributaries of the Red River. Deeply incised 120-mile-long canyon cuts through richly colored deposits of claystone, sandstone, and mudstone. Rolling Plains prairie varies in composition from short-grass on rim to mixed- and tallgrass on canyon floor. A National Natural Landmark.

From Canyon, go east 12 miles on Highway 217.

4 Caprock Canyons State Park

15,313 acres, TPWD, (806) 455-1492

Impressive erosional landscapes along Red River drainages. Park encompasses 600-acre restored mixed-grass prairie and herds of Southern Plains bison and pronghorn antelope as well as miles of multi-use rail-to-trail conversion.

From Quitaque, go north 3.5 miles on FM 1065.

5 Copper Breaks State Park

1,899 acres, TPWD, *(940) 839-4331*
Rugged landscape steeped in the history of the Comanche and Kiowa. Good mixed-grass prairie can be seen in the backcountry of the park. Restored grassland is at the entrance.
From Quanah, go south 12 miles on Highway 6.

6 Monahans Sandhills State Park

3,840 acres, TPWD, *(915) 943-2092*
Active and stabilized dune fields on southern fringe of the High Plains. The deep sands hold water that supports scattered tallgrass prairie interspersed with one of the shortest oak forests in North America.
From Monahans, go northeast 5 miles on I-20 to Park Road 41 (Exit 86).

BLACKLAND PRAIRIE/CROSS TIMBERS

The Blackland Prairie is a narrow strip of dark, alkaline clays stretching roughly from north of Dallas almost to San Antonio. This area once supported 12 million acres of primarily tallgrass prairie, of which less than 5,000 acres remain. The Cross Timbers is a distinctive swath of oak woodland, prairie savanna, and glade extending from southeastern Kansas through the heart of Oklahoma into north central Texas. It forms an ecotone between eastern deciduous forest and southern Great Plains grasslands. Clearing of the Cross Timbers for grazing, suburban development, and other twenty-first-century pursuits is obliterating an ancient landscape.

7 LBJ National Grasslands

20,250 acres, USDA-FS, *(940) 627-5475*
Patchwork of restored grasslands and hardwood forests northwest of Dallas–Fort Worth in gently rolling hills of the Grand Prairie and Western Cross Timbers ecosystems. Wide-open spaces on fringe of the megalopolis attract horseback riders, mountain bikers, hunters, and boaters.

Maps and information available from the district office, 1400 N. Highway 81/287, in Decatur.

8 Caddo National Grasslands

17,785 acres, USDA-FS, (940) 627-5475

Three scattered sites near the towns of Bonham and Paris set aside in the 1930s to control erosion in the Red River watershed. Landscapes surrounding several constructed lakes reflect the grasslands and hardwood forests typical of the Eastern Cross Timbers and Blackland Prairie ecosystems.

Maps and information available from the district office, 1400 N. Highway 81/287, in Decatur.

9 Cedar Hill State Park

1,826 acres, TPWD, (972) 291-3900

Urban nature preserve on the edge of Dallas–Fort Worth harbors five remnant tracts of tallgrass prairie.

From Cedar Hill (10 miles southwest of Dallas), take FM 1382 off Highway 67, then go north 2.5 miles.

10 Tallgrass Prairie/Blackland Prairie Complex

Approximately 1,300 acres in scattered locations, private ownership and TNC, (210) 224-8774

TNC partnership with private landowners to protect and restore remaining examples of tallgrass and blackland prairies at a handful of locations in north central Texas, the largest of which is the 1,068-acre Clymer Meadow Preserve west of Greenville. Other sites are near towns of Paris and Marlin.

Access limited to research and volunteer activities. Call TNC for information.

THE TRANS-PECOS

The Trans-Pecos (the area of Texas west of the Pecos River) is better known for spectacular desert and mountain vistas than for grass.

However, its semidesert grasslands constitute one of the largest contiguous grasslands in the U.S. Much of the land is privately owned. Recommended routes traversing exceptional landscapes include Highway 62/180 (Hueco Mountains–Cornudas Scenic Drive), Highway 67 (Marfa to Shafter), and Highway 385 (Marathon to Fort Stockton). Public access is as follows.

11 Davis Mountains State Park

2,709 acres, TPWD, (915) 426-3337
Lovely pine- and oak-covered mountain range, the most extensive in Texas, and see-forever expanse of plains grasslands in the Chihuahuan Desert.

From Fort Davis, go north 1 mile on Highway 17, then west 3 miles on Highway 118.

12 Big Bend Ranch State Park

280,280 acres, TPWD, (915) 229-3416
A wild chunk of Chihuahuan Desert that includes some of the most remote territory in the Southwest.

Permits are required to enter park. Obtain at Fort Leaton State Historical Park, 4 miles east of Presidio on FM 170, or Barton Warnock Environmental Education Center, 1 mile east of Lajitas on FM 170.

13 Big Bend National Park

801,163 acres, NPS, (915) 477-2251
The Chisos Mountains, completely surrounded by the park, rise up majestically from the Chihuahuan Desert floor. From the canyons of the Rio Grande to the immense stretches of desert to the peaks of the Chisos, the park provides dramatic opportunities to appreciate its diverse plant and animal life and its geological formations.

From Marathon, go 70 miles south on Highway 385 to park headquarters at Panther Junction.

THE EDWARDS PLATEAU

This region of west central Texas, also known as the Hill Country, leaves an impression of ruggedness but in fact is a fragile landscape of shallow soils atop massive deposits of limestone. It is a favorite escape of city dwellers, especially from nearby San Antonio and Austin, who typically go to enjoy its crystalline, bald cypress–lined rivers and streams. Its lovely grasslands, often interspersed with oak woodlands, have suffered a number of assaults, including nineteenth-century overstocking of goats, sheep, and cattle, an invasion of exotic grasses, suppression of fire, subdivision for small-acreage ranchettes, and urban sprawl.

14 Enchanted Rock State Natural Area

1,643 acres, TPWD, *(915) 247-3903*
Grasslands intermixed with mesquite and oak woodlands against exquisite backdrop of 400-foot-high pink granite batholith, the tip of an extensive underground block. A National Natural Landmark.
From Fredericksburg, go north 18 miles on Ranch Road 965.

15 Guadalupe River State Park

1,938 acres, TPWD, *(830) 438-2656*
Fine examples of oak woodlands intermingled with prairie, enhanced by bald cypress on the banks of the Guadalupe.
From Boerne, go east 13 miles on Highway 46, then north on Park Road 31.

16 Hill Country State Natural Area

5,370 acres, TPWD, *(830) 796-4413*
Former Merrick Bar-O-Ranch on West Verde Creek encompasses oak woods and grasslands amid rocky hills and canyons. Areas accessible to public, however, are dominated by KR bluestem, an exotic Asian species introduced at the King Ranch in 1930s as a forage grass and now widespread across Texas.
From Bandera, go south on Highway 173 to edge of town, cross Medina River, go .25 mile, then take Highway 1077 southwest for 10 miles.

17 Kerr Wildlife Management Area

6,493 acres, TPWD, (830) 238-4483
Situated at the scenic headwaters of the North Fork of the Guadalupe River, this former grassland savanna (prior to European settlement) is the site of various management practices geared to restoring a portion of the original landscape.

From Kerrville, go west on Highway 27 to Ingram, continue west on Highway 39 to Hunt, then go northwest 12 miles on Ranch Road 1340.

THE TEXAS GULF PRAIRIES

The 9 million acres that originally comprised the Texas Gulf prairies formed a vast swath of tallgrass and oak savanna. The pancake-flat, poorly drained grassland segues into squishy marshes—some fresh, others salty—and barrier islands fringed by sand dunes. Auto routes that impart a feeling for the surreal simplicity of the coastal prairie landscape include Highway 239 (Goliad to Tivoli) and the incomparable drive on Highway 77 through the King Ranch, also known as the Wild Horse Desert (Kingsville to Raymondville). Public access is as follows.

18 Anahuac National Wildlife Refuge

Approximately 34,000 acres, USFWS, (409) 267-3337
Beautiful vista of coastal prairie and marshes where presence of American alligator adds an extra thrill to the prairie-watching experience. The auto tour around Shoveler Pond affords views of wintering snow geese; willows and salt cedars provide a refuge for migrating birds in the spring.

From Houston, go east on I-10 across the Old River Bridge to Exit 812 (Anahuac-Hankamer), then south 2 miles on Highway 61 to intersection with FM 562. Continue south 8.3 miles on FM 562, then east 4 miles on FM 1985 to refuge entrance.

19 Armand Bayou Coastal Preserve and Nature Center

2,800 acres, Armand Bayou Nature Center, (281) 474-2551

A natural gem in the Houston metroplex encompassing remnant coastal prairies and marshes, wooded streams, prairie potholes, and brackish bayous feeding into West Galveston Bay. Extensive educational offerings available.

From Houston, go south on I-45 to Bay Area Boulevard (Exit 26). Go east 7 miles to preserve entrance at 8500 Bay Area Boulevard on south side of road.

20 Galveston Island State Park

1,930 acres, TPWD, (409) 737-1222

Extensive coastal prairie and wetlands on the western, wilder end of Galveston Island. Park has restored 750 acres of salt marsh.

From Galveston, take I-45 to Galveston Island and exit at 61st Street (Spur 342), going south until street intersects with Seawall Boulevard (FM 3005). Go west 10 miles to park entrance.

21 Attwater Prairie Chicken National Wildlife Refuge

8,385 acres, USFWS, (979) 234-3021

Refuge is large enough to give visitors a glimmer of what the original coastal prairie must have looked, sounded, and smelled like. Today, less than 1 percent remains, and the Attwater, a slightly smaller form of the greater prairie-chicken, is dangerously close to extinction. A National Natural Landmark.

From Eagle Lake, go 7 miles northeast on FM 3013.

22 Texas City Prairie Preserve

2,303 acres, TNC, (210) 224-8774

Coastal prairie remnant overlooking Galveston Bay in Texas City. One of the last three remaining sites that support wild Attwater prairie-chickens.

Access limited to research and volunteer activities. Call TNC for information.

23 Clive Runnells Family Mad Island Marsh Preserve

7,048 acres, TNC, (361) 972-2559

Tallgrass coastal prairie mingling with salt marsh in heart of the wintering grounds of the endangered whooping crane.

Preserve is southeast of Collegeport off FM 1095. Access limited to research and volunteer activities. Call TNC for information.

24 Matagorda Island State Park and Wildlife Management Area

43,893 acres, TPWD, USFWS, (361) 983-2215

Magnificent dunes, marshes, and coastal prairie unfurl across a 38-mile-long barrier island accessible only by boat. Area is home to many threatened and endangered species including brown pelicans, whooping cranes, and the Texas diamondback terrapin. Ferry to island operates Thursday through Sunday.

Park headquarters at intersection of 16th and Maples Streets in Port O'Connor. Contact park office for ferry schedules, fees, and other information.

25 Aransas National Wildlife Refuge

59,700 acres, USFWS, (361) 286-3559

Famed wintering ground of the last wild flock of whooping cranes, the refuge also harbors extensive coastal prairie, live oak mottes, and tidal marshes.

From Rockport, go north 20 miles on Highway 35, east 9 miles on Highway 774, then south 7 miles on FM 2040 to refuge entrance.

26 Welder Wildlife Refuge

7,800 acres, Rob and Bessie Welder Wildlife Foundation,
(361) 364-2643

A lovely gesture of philanthropy that protects exquisite wetland and coastal prairie landscape and supports ongoing wildlife research in the context of an operating ranch. Refuge was established in 1954 on portion of Spanish land grant that had been in the Welder family since 1832. The refuge is open to the public every Thursday afternoon or by appointment.

From Sinton, go northeast 8 miles on Highway 77. Refuge entrance is on east side of road.

27 King Ranch

825,000 acres, (361) 592-8055

The legendary King Ranch, one of the last unbroken stretches of coastal prairie, offers an assortment of nature tours, geared primarily to birdwatchers, as well as customized tours.

For information, contact the King Ranch Visitor Center, Highway 141 West, P.O. Box 1090, Kingsville TX 78364.

28 Laguna Atascosa National Wildlife Refuge

45,187 acres, USFWS, (956) 748-3607

Wild, remote, starkly beautiful coastal prairie interlaced with resacas (channels formerly flooded by the Rio Grande), wetlands, and subtropical thorn forest. This southernmost U.S. waterfowl refuge provides sanctuary for two species of endangered tropical cats, the small, stealthy ocelot and the long-bodied, long-tailed jaguarundi. Very high biological diversity, including more than four hundred species of birds.

From Harlingen, take FM 106 east 14 miles past Rio Hondo to intersection of FM 106 and Buena Vista Road, then north 3 miles to visitors' center.

ABBREVIATIONS

CCB	County Conservation Board
CCFPD	Cook County Forest Preserve District
IDNR	In Illinois chapter: Illinois Department of Natural Resources; in Iowa chapter: Iowa Department of Natural Resources
KDWP	Kansas Department of Wildlife and Parks
MC	Manitoba Conservation
MCCD	McHenry County Conservation District
MDC	Missouri Department of Conservation
MDNR	Missouri Department of Natural Resources
MPF	Missouri Prairie Foundation
NAS	National Audubon Society
NDPRD	North Dakota Parks and Recreation Department
NPS	National Park Service
PC	Parks Canada
SNA	Scientific and Natural Areas
TNC	The Nature Conservancy
TPWD	Texas Parks and Wildlife Department
USACE	U.S. Army Corps of Engineers
USDA-FS	U.S. Department of Agriculture, Forest Service
USFWS	U.S. Fish and Wildlife Service
WCFPD	Will County Forest Preserve District

RECOMMENDED READINGS, WEB SITES, AND ORGANIZATIONS

This list contains my favorite prairie literature, regional guidebooks, and Web sites. It also includes contact information for groups involved in various aspects of prairie conservation and restoration and sustainable grassland practices. It is not intended to be a comprehensive grassland bibliography.

GENERAL

Atlas and Gazetteer Series. DeLorme. Order via http://www.delorme.com (accessed July 23, 2003). DeLorme atlases are available for every state covered in this guide. They are very useful and user-friendly.

Brown, Lauren. *The Audubon Society Nature Guides: Grasslands*. Alfred A. Knopf, 1985.

Frazier, Ian. *Great Plains*. Farrar Straus & Giroux, 1989.

Grassland Heritage Foundation. http://www.grasslandheritage.org (accessed July 23, 2003). Devoted to prairie preservation and education.

Grasslands for Tomorrow. http://www.ducks.org/conservation/Projects/ GreatPlains/GreatPlainsProjects/GrasslandsForTomorrowIndex.asp (accessed July 23, 2003). An initiative of Ducks Unlimited on the Central and Northern Great Plains to protect and restore grasslands on public lands and on private lands of willing landowners.

Great Plains Restoration Council. http://www.gprc.org (accessed July 23, 2003). Dedicated to advancing the Buffalo Commons concept proposed in 1987 by geographers Frank and Deborah Popper. The primary goals are to reconnect a network of prairie landscapes from Canada to Mexico and to restore historic free-ranging bison within this virtually unfenced terrain.

Johnsgard, Paul A. *Prairie Birds: Fragile Splendor in the Great Plains*. University Press of Kansas, 2001.

Licht, Daniel S. *Ecology and Economics of the Great Plains*. University of Nebraska Press, 1997.

Long Term Ecological Research Network. http://www.lternet.edu (accessed July 23, 2003). An effort of the National Science Foundation to study large-scale ecological processes over prolonged time periods in an array of ecosystems. One tallgrass site is part of the study: Konza Prairie in Kansas.

McClaran, Mitchel P., and Thomas R. Van Devender, eds. *The Desert Grassland*. University of Arizona Press, 1995.

National Audubon Society. http://www.audubon.org (accessed July 23, 2003). "Audubon's mission is to conserve and restore natural ecosystems, focusing on birds, other wildlife, and their habitats for the benefit of humanity and the earth's biological diversity."

National Park Foundation. http://www.nationalparks.org (accessed July 23, 2003). "The mission of the National Park Foundation, chartered by Congress, is to strengthen the enduring connection between the American people and their National Parks."

National Parks Conservation Association. http://www.npca.org (accessed July 23, 2003). Created in 1919 as a watchdog for the National Park Service, today NPCA partners with the federal government and other national, regional, and local groups to help safeguard the U.S. park system.

National Park Service. http://www.nps.gov (accessed July 23, 2003). Comprehensive guide to national parks, natural landmarks, educational opportunities, publications, and more.

National Wildlife Federation. http://www.nwf.org (accessed July 23, 2003). "Working to make policy makers, the public, teachers and school children aware of the vast beauty our nation's grasslands hold and of the critical importance of acting now to save them." Visit this site for information on the National Grasslands program and the Dakota Prairie Grasslands.

The Nature Conservancy. http://www.nature.org (accessed July 23, 2003). Since 1951, dedicated to preserving "the plants, animals and natural communities that represent the diversity of life on Earth by protecting the lands and waters they need to survive."

Northern Prairies Land Trust. http://www.northernprairies.org (accessed July 23, 2003). Protecting prairies in South Dakota and Nebraska.

Northern Prairie Wildlife Research Center. http://www.npwrc.usgs.gov (accessed July 23, 2003). An excellent source of information on grassland resources and conservation.

Partners in Flight. http://www.blm.gov/wildlife/pifplans.htm (accessed July 23, 2003). PIF's *Physiographic Areas Plans* provides concise descriptions of the physiographic areas that define the prairie states and thus is an excellent source for gaining an increased understanding of the landscapes mentioned in this guide. This publication also discusses the conservation needs of each area. Visit http://www.PartnersInFlight.org for general information on this organization.

Prairie Passage. http://www.dot.state.mn.us/environment/whatsnew/ prairie_passage.html (accessed July 23, 2003). A partnership to promote increased public appreciation of North America's prairies. Its efforts are focused on establishing a network of signed routes that lead travelers along roadways with significant prairie resources. The routes, which will ultimately extend from Canada to Mexico, are marked with signs with the image of a prairie coneflower. Minnesota, Iowa, Missouri, Kansas, Oklahoma, and Texas are the current partners in Prairie Passage. Funding is by the Departments of Transportation in these states and by the Federal Highway Administration. The program is also working to protect and restore native wildflowers and grasses along roadsides. For information, contact Prairie Passage Coordinator, Minnesota Department of Transportation, 395 John Ireland Boulevard, Box 620, St. Paul MN 55155, (651) 284-3765.

Prairies Forever. http://www.prairies.org (accessed July 23, 2003). "Dedicated to promoting the ecological and cultural significance of the American prairie through education, outreach, and public engagement."

Sierra Club. http://www.sierraclub.org (accessed July 23, 2003). America's oldest and largest grassroots environmental group.

The Smithsonian Guides to Natural America. Smithsonian Books and Random House, 1995, 1996. Pertinent volumes: *The Northern Rockies, The Southern Rockies, The Northern Plains, The Heartland, The South Central States.*

Trails and Grasslands. http://www.trailsandgrasslands.org (accessed July 23, 2003). A personal tour of grassland road trips and hiking trails.

U.S. Department of Agriculture, Forest Service. http://www.fs.fed.us (accessed July 23, 2003).

U.S. Fish and Wildlife Service. http://www.fws.gov (accessed July 23, 2003).

Upham, Warren. *The Glacial Lake Agassiz.* Government Printing Office, 1895. http://www.lib.ndsu.nodak.edu/govdocs/text/lakeagassiz (accessed July 23, 2003). Classic geological description of the immense landform associated with prairie ecosystems in Canada, North Dakota, and Minnesota.

Weaver, J. E. *North American Prairie.* Johnsen Publishing Co., 1954. A classic text by a pioneer in grassland ecology, long out of print but worth seeking.

Webb, Walter Prescott. *The Great Plains.* 1931. Reprint, University of Nebraska Press, 1981.

World Wildlife Federation. http://www.wwf.org (accessed July 23, 2003). In the words of WWF founder, Peter Scott, in 1961, "We shan't save all we should like to, but we shall save a great deal more than if we had never tried."

CANADA

Parks Canada. http://www.parkscanada.gc.ca/default_flash.html (accessed July 24, 2003). Complete information on national parks, historic sites, conservation areas, etc.

Stegner, Wallace. *Wolf Willow: A History, a Story, and a Memory of the Last Plains Frontier.* Penguin Classics, 2001.

THE DAKOTAS

Dakota Prairie Grasslands. http://www.fs.fed.us/r1/dakotaprairie (accessed July 24, 2003). Information on the 1.2 million acres of national grasslands in the Dakotas. The federal agency is charged with developing a long-term management plan for these prairies.

Hasselstrom, Linda. *Feels Like Far: A Rancher's Life on the Great Plains.* Lyons Press, 1999.

National Wildlife Federation, Dakota Prairie Grasslands. http://www.nwf. org/dakotaprairiegrasslands (accessed December 8, 2003). Provides a link to a special report, "Restoring the Prairie: Mending the Sacred Hoop," which discusses prairie restoration on the Cheyenne River Sioux Reservation and the conservation possibilities for grasslands and wildlife across America.

Norris, Kathleen. *Dakota: A Spiritual Geography.* Ticknor and Fields, 1993.

North Dakota Parks and Recreation Department. http://www.ndparks.com (accessed July 24, 2003).

O'Brien, Dan. *Buffalo for the Broken Heart: Restoring Life to a Black Hills Ranch.* Random House, 2001.

South Dakota Department of Game, Fish and Parks. http://www.state. sd.us/gfp (accessed July 24, 2003).

ILLINOIS

Chicago Wilderness, http://www.chicagowilderness.org, and *Chicago Wilderness Magazine*, http://www.chicagowildernessmag.org (both accessed July 24, 2003). Command central for information about remnant prairies in metro Chicago.

Cronon, William. *Nature's Metropolis: Chicago and the Great West.* W. W. Norton, 1991.

Illinois Department of Natural Resources, Illinois Nature Preserves Commission. http://www.dnr.state.il.us/INPC/Directory (accessed July 24, 2003). Online list of state nature preserves.

Illinois Natural History Survey. http://www.inhs.uiuc.edu/ (accessed July 24, 2003). The mission of the INHS is to "investigate and document the biological resources of Illinois and other areas, and to acquire and provide natural history information that can be used to promote the common understanding, conservation, and management of these resources."

Inventory of Resource Rich Areas in Illinois. http://www.inhs.uiuc.edu/ cwe/rra/rra.html (accessed July 24, 2003). Summaries of significant natural landscapes in Illinois.

McFall, Don, and Jean Karnes, eds. *A Directory of Illinois Nature Preserves.* 2 vols. Illinois Department of Natural Resources, Division of Natural Heritage, 1995.

Natural Land Institute. http://www.naturalland.org (accessed July 24, 2003). Regional land trust that preserves natural areas in Illinois and southern Wisconsin.

Packard, Stephen, and Cornelia F. Mutel, eds. *The Tallgrass Restoration Handbook: For Prairies, Savannas, and Woodlands.* Island Press, 1997.

ParkLands Foundation. http://www.parklands.org (accessed July 24, 2003). Focuses on preservation, restoration, and maintenance of natural lands in central Illinois.

Save the Prairie Society. http://www.savetheprairiesociety.org (accessed July 24, 2003). Enthusiastic group of Chicago-based prairie activists whose first and central achievement has been the protection of Wolf Road Prairie.

Tallgrass Prairie in Illinois. http://www.inhs.uiuc.edu/~kenr/tallgrass.html (accessed July 24, 2003). Excellent resource for prairie information.

IOWA

Christiansen, Paul, and Mark Müller. *An Illustrated Guide to Iowa Prairie Plants*. University of Iowa Press, 1999.

Dinsmore, Stephen J., et al. *Iowa Wildlife Viewing Guide*. Falcon Press Publishing Co., 1995.

Herzberg, Ruth, and John Pearson. *The Guide to Iowa's State Preserves*. University of Iowa Press, 2001.

Iowa Department of Natural Resources. http://www.state.ia.us/parks (accessed July 24, 2003). Online list of state preserves.

Iowa Natural Heritage Foundation. http://www.inhf.org (accessed July 24, 2003). Protects Iowa's land, water, and wildlife "for those who follow."

Iowa Prairie Network. http://www.iowaprairienetwork.org (accessed July 24, 2003). This organization has a terrific newsletter and leads many field trips to remnant Iowa prairies.

Mutel, Cornelia F. *Fragile Giants: A Natural History of the Loess Hills*. University of Iowa Press, 1989.

Prior, Jean C. *Landforms of Iowa*. University of Iowa Press, 1991.

Neal Smith National Wildlife Refuge, Friends of the Prairie Learning Center. http://www.tallgrass.org (accessed July 24, 2003). Information on the largest reconstruction project for tallgrass prairie in the U.S.

KANSAS

Buchanan, Rex, ed. *Geology: An Introduction to Landscapes, Rocks, Minerals, and Fossils*. University Press of Kansas, 1984.

Great Plains Nature Center. http://www.gpnc.org (accessed July 24, 2003). Wichita-based nature center that promotes appreciation of Great Plains flora and fauna.

Gress, Bob, and George Potts. *Watching Kansas Wildlife*. University Press of Kansas, 1993.

Kansas Department of Wildlife and Parks. http://www.kdwp.state.ks.us (accessed July 24, 2003).

The Land Institute. http://www.landinstitute.org (accessed July 24, 2003). Dedicated to using the prairie as a model of ecological stability to devise a new form of agriculture that sustains natural resources and rural communities.

Least Heat-Moon, William. *PrairyErth (A Deep Map)*. Houghton Mifflin, 1991.

Natural Kansas. http://www.naturalkansas.org (accessed July 24, 2003). A guide to visiting natural areas of Kansas.

Reichman, O. J. *Konza Prairie: A Tallgrass Natural History*. University Press of Kansas, 1987.

MINNESOTA

Chapman, Kim Alan, Adelheid Fischer, and Mary Kinsella Ziegenhagen. *Valley of Grass: Tallgrass Prairie and Parkland of the Red River Region*. Star Press of St. Cloud and The Nature Conservancy, 1998.

Gruchow, Paul. *Journal of a Prairie Year*. University of Minnesota Press, 1985.

A Guide to Minnesota's Scientific and Natural Areas. Available from the Minnesota DNR Gift Shop, (651) 228-9165, or Minnesota's Bookstore, (651) 297-3000. Information also available on MDNR SNA Web site, http:// www.dnr.state.mn.us/snas/index.html (accessed July 24, 2003).

A Guide to The Nature Conservancy's Preserves in Minnesota, 2000 Edition. Available from TNC, 1313 5th Street SE, Minneapolis MN 55414, (612) 331-0750.

Minnesota Department of Natural Resources, Scientific and Natural Areas Program. http:// www.dnr.state.mn.us/snas/index.html (accessed July 24, 2003). Online site descriptions.

MISSOURI

Directory of Missouri Natural Areas. Missouri Department of Conservation, Missouri Natural Areas Committee, 1996. Information also available on MDC MNAP Web site (noted below).

Missouri Department of Conservation, Missouri Natural Areas Program. Site descriptions listed online at http://www.conservation.state.mo.us/ areas/natareas (accessed July 24, 2003).

Missouri Department of Natural Resources. http://www.dnr.state.mo.us/ homednr.htm (accessed July 24, 2003).

Missouri Prairie Foundation. http://www.moprairie.org (accessed July 24, 2003). Vigorous land trust devoted to protecting native prairie tracts in Missouri.

NEBRASKA

Johnsgard, Paul A. *This Fragile Land: A Natural History of the Nebraska Sandhills.* University of Nebraska Press, 1995.

Sandoz, Mari. *The Buffalo Hunters.* 1954. Reprint, University of Nebraska Press, 1978.

Sandoz, Mari. *Love Song to the Plains.* 1961. Reprint, University of Nebraska Press, 1986.

Prairie Plains Resource Institute. http://www.prairieplains.org (accessed July 24, 2003). This grass-roots organization, a leader in prairie restoration, has developed methods for restoring robust prairies with a high-diversity seed mix of grasses and wildflowers. Most of its restoration efforts are focused on land along the Platte River corridor in south central Nebraska.

Sandhills Task Force. http://www.sandhillstaskforce.org (accessed July 24, 2003). An innovative group of ranchers and conservation agencies working to promote research, education, technical assistance, and on-the-ground conservation practices within the Sandhills' ranching community.

OKLAHOMA

Ancient Cross Timbers Project. http://www.uark.edu/misc/xtimber (accessed July 24, 2003). Dedicated to surveying and preserving this vanishing ancient landscape.

Oklahoma Tourism and Recreation Department. http://tourism.state.ok.us/ (accessed July 24, 2003).

TEXAS

Hatch, Stephan L., Joseph L. Schuster, and D. Lynn Drawe. *Grasses of the Texas Gulf Prairies and Marshes.* Texas A&M University Press, 1999.

Katy Prairie Conservancy. http://www.katyprairie.org (accessed July 24, 2003). Nonprofit organization working to protect 40,000 acres of increasingly threatened coastal prairie west of Houston.

Moulton, Dan, and John Jacob. *Texas Coastal Wetlands Guide.* Free publication available from the Texas Parks and Wildlife Department, Coastal

Conservation Branch, 3000 S. I-35, Suite 320, Austin, TX 78704, (512) 912–7190.

Native Prairies Association of Texas. http://www.texasprairie.org (accessed July 24, 2003). Nonprofit organization involved in grassland conservation and restoration. Sponsors numerous events and field trips.

Texas Parks and Wildlife Department. http://www.tpwd.state.tx.us/ (accessed July 24, 2003). See http://www.tpwd.state.tx.us/nature/plant/ grascom.htm for specific information on natural areas including grasslands.

INDEX

Comprehensive Index

Geographic Index